HENRY, RICHARD, AND MIKE **BLACKABY**

CLAUDE V. **KING**

EXPERIENCING

GOD

Knowing & Doing
the Will of God

Lifeway Press® • Brentwood, Tennessee

Published by Lifeway Press®
© 2022 Henry Blackaby, Richard Blackaby, and Claude King
Reprinted July 2022

For further information about the Blackaby's ministry contact Blackaby Ministries International; P.O. Box 1035; Jonesboro, GA 30237; 770.471.2332; www.blackaby.org

The illustrations of the authors are written solely from their personal viewpoints. Others who were involved, if given the opportunity, could write different and more complete accounts.

ISBN 978-1-0877-5786-5 • Item 005836246

Dewey decimal classification: 231
Subject heading: GOD—WILL

To order additional copies of this resource, write to Lifeway Resources Customer Service; 200 Powell Place, Suite 100; Brentwood, TN 37027; fax 615-251-5933; phone toll free 800-458-2772; order online at Lifeway.com; or email orderentry@lifeway.com.

Printed in the United States of America.

Adult Ministry Publishing
Lifeway Resources
200 Powell Place, Suite 100
Brentwood, TN 37027

CONTENTS

EXPERIENCING

GOD

ENROLLMENT/ATTENDANCE

Leader: _____

Name	Session (Check Attendance)												
	Intro.	1	2	3	4	5	6	7	8	9	10	11	12
1.													
2.													
3.													
4.													
5.													
6.													
7.													
8.													
9.													
10.													

LEADING A SMALL GROUP STUDY OF
EXPERIENCING GOD

For an introduction to *Experiencing God,* read pages 8–10 in the member book. Read that introduction before you continue reading this overview.

    Experiencing God is not just a book for reading. It is part of a learning system designed to teach the content material and help people move into a deeper relationship with God. To achieve this goal, learners should utilize every element of the learning system. They need to complete the self-study in the workbook during the week. Then learners need to meet in a small group (8 to 10 people maximum) to review, discuss questions that arise, share personal experiences and insights, pray for one another, and apply the truths to life. Access to video teaching sessions by Richard and Mike Blackaby are included with the purchase of each *Experiencing God* member book. These teachings will enrich the study and encourage participants in the study.

    Experiencing God and other similar courses are often offered through a church's discipleship-training program. If your church does not have an ongoing discipleship program, you can still offer the course. In fact, some churches use this course to start or revitalize their training of disciples. If you would like to learn more about courses like *Experiencing God*, visit *www.lifeway.com/discipleship.*

NOTE: Page numbers identified in this leader guide refer to the *Experiencing God* member book. When the page number refers to this leader guide, it will be preceded by LG, as in (LG p. #).

www.lifeway.com/discipleship

HOW TO USE THIS LEADER GUIDE

This leader guide is designed to assist you in preparing for and conducting the small group sessions each week. The remainder of "Leading a Small group Study of *Experiencing God*" will prepare you to lead the course, enlist participants, and prepare for the small group sessions. LG pages 15–55 provide step-by-step procedures for conducting an introductory session and 12 group sessions. Each group-session plan includes three parts:

1. *"Before the Session."* This section includes actions for you to complete prior to the group session. Boxes (❑) are provided for you to check as you complete each action. I have done my best to provide sessions that require a minimum of leader preparation so you can give yourself to prayer and personal spiritual preparation. If you adapt the lesson plans or create activities of your own, you will need to secure any resources that are required for these activities.

2. *"During the Session."* This section provides learning activities for you to use in conducting the group session. The activities suggested in each session follow a similar pattern. The first segments focus on reviewing the unit content, sharing personal experiences and responses to that content, and praying for concerns related to the sharing. An optional singing time is also suggested. The viewing and discussion of the video teaching sessions is recommended for the last part of the session. If, for some reason, time limits how much of the session you can complete, the most important part is the interpersonal sharing that takes place at the beginning of the session.

3. *"After the Session."* A standard guide for evaluating your experience in each session is provided on LG page 63. Each week you are encouraged to think about your group members and identify one or more who may need a personal contact from you. I hope you will not neglect this aspect of your ministry. Your primary assign-

ment in this study is to help people grow in Christ, not just teach knowledge. Invest your time in people, and you will reap a valuable reward!

YOUR ROLE AS A SMALL GROUP LEADER

You may be asking yourself, *Why did I agree to teach this study? I need to learn how to know and do God's will myself.* Your role in this small group study is not that of a teacher. You are a leader of learning activities. You are a facilitator of the group learning process. If you sense God has led you to accept this assignment, you can trust Him to equip and enable you to accomplish the task. As you will learn, you are an instrument through which God wants to do His work. Depend on Him and "pray continually" (1 Thess. 5:17).

Group members will spend as much as two or three hours studying each unit of *Experiencing God*. The Holy Spirit will be their Teacher. The content and learning activities will help members learn the basic truths and principles during the week. Your job is to help them review what they have learned; share with one another what God has revealed of Himself, His purposes, and His ways; and apply these truths to their personal lives, their families, their work, and their church life.

Group members may ask some questions you cannot answer. Expect them. Welcome them. In these cases apply what you are learning. When you do not have the answer (or maybe even when you do), encourage the group to join you in praying and searching the Scriptures. Together ask God to guide you to His answer and to His perspective. Then trust Him to do it. When God sends the answer through one or more group members, you all will know more of God and His ways because of the experience.

EFFECTIVE GROUP SIZE

Jesus preached to large crowds, but He did most of His discipleship training with a group of 12. He was even more intimate with three of His disciples who would be key leaders in the New Testament church. You need to provide a learning environment in which God can do His best work in participants' lives. Participants need to be in a small group where they can ask questions, share personal experiences, and pray intimately with brothers and sisters in Christ. They do not need to be in a crowd where they would be more of a spectator than a participant. Therefore, provide a small group for each 8 to 10 participants. If more than 10 persons are interested, provide for multiple groups in order to create the best possible learning environment.

In "During the Session" each activity has a recommended grouping for the activity. I have recommended the size of the sharing group based on the content to be shared and the amount of time available. You may decide to use different groupings within your small group, and that is OK. If you make a change, however, evaluate what members will share, how much time you have, and what size group would provide for maximum participation by members.

Here is a description of the terms used for group work:
- **Small group** refers to a group of 8 to 10 persons including the small group leader.
- **Quads** refers to 4 persons (a quad). Depending on the size of your group, each quad may actually have 3 or 4 members. For instance, if you have 8 members, you would have 2 quads of 4 each. For 10 members I recommend 2 "quads" of 3 members and 1 quad of 4. If you have 6 members, divide the members equally. You should participate in quad activities. When you divide into quads, verbally give the assignment to all members. You may need to assign one member in

each quad as the leader. During "Sharing Time" some of the topics are listed in the bottom margin of the session page at the end of each unit. You may invite members to turn to that page to guide the sharing time.

- **Pairs** refers to two persons working together. If you have an odd number of participants, one "pair" will need to have three members, or one person can work with you as a pair.
- **Large group** is reserved for activities in which more than one small group joins together to view the video teachings session. These video teaching sessions are included with the purchase of every member book, and may be viewed on Lifeway's video on demand platform.

LARGE GROUP VIDEO TEACHING VIEWING

Many churches may have more than one small group studying *Experiencing God* at the same time. While every person with a member book will receive a unique access code to view the video teaching sessions on Lifeway's video on demand platform, you may choose to watch the teaching sessions as a large group. If you would prefer to use DVDs instead of the video on demand application, you may purchase the *Experiencing God DVD Set* (item 005836990).

If all the groups plan to view the video teaching sessions at the same time, you may want to schedule a large group time to view these sessions. Your pastor or another assigned leader can guide the viewing of the teaching sessions. You will still want to divide into your small groups to discuss and process the unit content.

If you must use this large group option to view the video teaching sessions, do not neglect the small group sessions. People will learn far more in a session in which each one must share, discuss, and struggle with the application of the spiritual truths. Small groups should remain the same throughout the course. One essential of *koinonia,* as you will learn, is that individuals must experience God in a real and personal way.

Access to video teaching sessions are included in each member book and can be viewed through Lifeway's video on demand application.

If you prefer, the video sessions are also sold as a DVD set.
Experiencing God DVD Set
Item 005836990
Available only from
(800) 458-2772

PREPARING FOR A GROUP STUDY

As a small group leader, you will need to prepare for the study, help enlist participants, guide the group sessions, and provide follow-up at the end of the study. The following suggestions should help you accomplish these tasks.

Determine the number of groups needed. Work with the pastor, the discipleship-training director, or others to determine how many individuals in your church want to study this course at this time. Any adult who has trusted Jesus Christ as Savior and Lord will benefit from this study. Survey your church members to determine the number of persons interested in a study to know and do the will of God. As mentioned earlier, you will need one group for every 10 members.

Enlist leaders. Each group will need its own leader. Your pastor may want to lead the first group and train 8 to 10 persons to cultivate leaders for future groups. If you need more leaders, he may want to take two or more groups through the course at different times during the week. Asking your pastor to lead the first group will ensure that he fully understands what *Experiencing God* is about and guides participants as they learn to respond to God. The study will also be inspiring and helpful in his own walk with the Lord. If your pastor is unable to lead this first group, enlist another spiritual leader in your church to guide the group. Because the leaders are lead learners, they do not necessarily need to have been through a group study prior to serving as a leader.

Order Resources

To order or inquire about resources, write to Lifeway Resources Customer Service; One Lifeway Plaza; Nashville, TN 37234; email orderentry@ lifeway.com; fax 615-251-5933; phone toll free 800-458-2772; or order online at Lifeway.com.

Pray that God will help you identify persons He wants to lead the groups. These leaders should be spiritually growing Christians and active church members. Leaders should have teachable spirits, an ability to relate well to people, a commitment to keep confidential information private, and a willingness to spend the time necessary to prepare for the sessions. Also look for people who possess skills for leading small group learning experiences.

Order resources. Resources should be ordered for the course a month or more before the first session. Although handling your order and shipping may take only a couple of weeks, leaders need time to prepare for the overview session and to enlist participants. Though you may not enlist participants until later, you can estimate the quantity needed by ordering 8 to 10 member books and one leader guide for each small group. Resources include:
- *Experiencing God: Knowing and Doing the Will of God* Bible study book with video access (item 005831467) for members
- *Experiencing God Leader Guide* (item 005085768) for leaders
- Optional—*Experiencing God: Knowing and Doing the Will of God* trade book (item 005834590)

Assets for conducting an Experiencing God Weekend and additional files and tools that may be helpful for leaders are located online at lifeway.com/egleader. Several of those files will be mentioned below as resources for guiding the small group sessions. For a detailed list of tools found online, consult page 13 of this book.

Provide notebooks. Each participant will need to keep a spiritual journal during the course. This journal will be organized during the introductory session (see LG pp. 15–18) or at least by the first group session. Decide whether you will provide the same kind of notebook for each person and include the cost in the fee for materials or whether you will ask each person to purchase a notebook or journal for use during the first week. One hundred pages should be adequate. Here are several suggestions:
- Three-ring binder with notebook paper and tab dividers
- Spiral-bound notebook, preferably with section dividers included
- Bound, diary-type book with blank pages

When you distribute the notebooks, point members to the instructions for keeping a spiritual journal on page 271 in the member book.

Set and collect fees. Course participants should be expected to pay for the cost of materials. If your church wants to share the cost, that is OK. I recommend, however, that participants pay at least part of the cost. Announce the fee at the times you enlist participants so they will not be embarrassed or surprised at the introductory session. You may want to provide full scholarships for those who would be unable to participate for financial reasons.

Prepare or secure additional resources. Much of your course preparation can be completed at one time. If you will complete the following actions, you will save time during the course for personal and spiritual preparation.
1. Make one copy of the following handouts for each member. You have permission to download these files and make copies for your group at lifeway.com/egleader
   Required:
   - Worksheets 1 and 2 on LG pages 61–62 (or download *Introductory_ Worksheets.pdf* from lifeway.com/egleader)
   Optional but helpful:

- "Scriptures for Meditation" (download *Scripture_Meditations.pdf* from lifeway.com/egleader)
- *Experiencing God* Course Evaluation" (download *EG_Evaluation.pdf* from lifeway.com/egleader)

2. Prepare the following posters.
   - *"Memorizing Scripture" poster.* Turn to "Help Members Memorize Scripture" (LG p. 11). Write the boldface instructions or key words on a poster for use in the introductory and first small group sessions (or print *Memorize_Scripture.pdf* from *lifeway.com/egleader*)
   - *"Seven Realities" poster.* On poster board draw a copy of the diagram on the inside back cover of the member book (or download and print *7_Realities_ Poster.pdf* from lifeway.com/egleader). You will use this poster throughout the course, so protect it.
   - *"God Speaks Through the Bible" and "God Speaks Through Prayer" diagram posters.* On poster board draw a copy of the diagrams on member book pages 104 and 108 (or download and print *Bible_Prayer_Poster.pdf* from lifeway.com/egleader)
   - *Unit posters.* Enlist group members to help prepare posters for use with each unit. Read the summary statements at the end of each day's lesson. Select three to five statements or Scriptures from each unit that seem to best capture the meaning of the unit for you. Write or print the statements on colored paper or card stock, construction paper, or ¼ sheets of poster board. (You may download and print posters using the file *Unit_Posters.pdf.* from lifeway.com/egleader) On the back of each poster write the unit number for use later. You may want to laminate the posters or spray them with clear plastic to protect them for repeated use.

3. If you plan to display copies of upcoming courses or discipleship-training resources in session 12, order them now. Before ordering, check with your church library or with an appropriate leader to learn whether your church already has copies that can be used for display.

4. Provide a dry-erase board or newsprint and suitable markers for use throughout the course. They will be needed on several occasions. Extra sheets of paper will be required in several sessions. Keep a supply in your meeting room.

Session Run Times	
Session 1	[18:47]
Session 2	[16:37]
Session 3	[18:28]
Session 4	[18:16]
Session 5	[17:34]
Session 6	[19:17]
Session 7	[16:59]
Session 8	[15:13]
Session 9	[15:14]
Session 10	[17:42]
Session 11	[12:32]
Session 12	[20:56]

Plan to use the video teaching sessions. Each *Experiencing God* member book includes an access code that grants members the ability to view the video teaching sessions featuring Richard and Mike Blackaby, which provide inspiring illustrations and additional explanation related to the corresponding units in the member book. This course has been designed to include the use of these 12 sessions. A viewer guide is included at the end of each unit in the member book with notes and Scripture references for the session. Each video teaching ends with a conversation between Richard and Mike that summarizes and applies the teaching.

Although the course is intended to include the use of the video teaching sessions, your group could complete the study of the member book and conduct the small group sessions without them.

Select a theme song. People learn much of their theology through songs or hymns. Music is also a valuable way to stimulate an affective (spiritual or emotional) response to the topics being studied. Consider selecting and singing (or playing a recorded version) of a theme song for this study. You might consider a hymn like "Trust and Obey" or a contemporary chorus like "Yes, Lord, Yes."

Decide when and where groups will meet. Groups may meet at the church, in homes, or at other convenient locations. You may want to offer group studies at a variety of times and locations so more people can participate.

Develop a time schedule. The recommended plans call for two-hour sessions each week. A typical session is divided like this:

> **Arrival Activity**—5 minutes
> **Singing/Special Music**—5 minutes
> **Unit Review**—15 minutes
> **Sharing Time**—30 minutes
> **Prayer Time**—15 minutes
> **Video Teaching Viewing and Discussion**—30 minutes
> **Closure**—5 minutes

If you have only one hour per week for your group sessions, select one of these options:

- *Recommended choice.* Take two weeks per unit of study. Complete individual study during the first week and use "Unit Review" and "Sharing Time" activities in the first session. Encourage individual review of the unit during the second week and use "Video Teaching Viewing and Discussion" in the second group session. This option would require 25 weeks—an introductory session and 24 group sessions.
- *Second choice.* Complete "Unit Review," "Sharing Time," and "Prayer Time" activities during your regular group session. Then offer "Video Teaching Viewing and Discussion" at an optional time for those who can attend. For instance, use Sunday evening for the first group session. Then offer the Video Teaching Sessions on Wednesday night before or after your weekly prayer service.
- *Third choice.* Encourage participants to use the access code and view the Video Teaching Sessions during the week.
- *Last resort.* Omit the video teaching sessions messages and adjust the remaining times and activities.

Enlist participants. Invite church leaders and other prospective participants to the introductory session (LG p. 15). This session will provide enough information for them to decide whether to participate in the study. At the end of the session, give those present an opportunity to enroll in the course. If persons are unwilling to make the necessary commitment to the individual and group study, ask them not to participate at this time. If you do not have enough groups (maximum of 10 members per group) to accommodate all who want to participate, enlist additional leaders from among those who plan to participate. Some leaders may even be willing to lead a second group at a different time during the week. This would require very little additional preparation. At the conclusion of the introductory session, set a date for the first session, distribute member books, and make assignments for the first unit.

Conduct an Experiencing God Weekend. Many churches have found that a weekend experience in which the *Experiencing God* message is introduced to the entire congregation generates more interest and willingness to commit to the study. Resources for planning and conducting an Experiencing God Weekend are available at lifeway.com/egleader.

Keep records. Use a copy of the enrollment/attendance form on LG page 4 for keeping your group records. Report your weekly attendance to the discipleship-training director or secretary.

HELP MEMBERS MEMORIZE SCRIPTURE

Some group members may not be skilled at memorizing Scripture. The following suggestions may be helpful. Write the boldface instructions on a poster for use in the introductory session and session 1 (or download and print *Memorize_Scripture.pdf* from lifeway.com/egleader). Be prepared to explain each suggestion.

1. **Write the verse and reference on a card.**
2. **Seek understanding.** Read the verse in its context. For instance, for John 15:5 you might read John 15:1-17. Study the verse and try to understand what it means.
3. **Read the verse aloud several times.**
4. **Learn to quote the verse one phrase at a time.** Divide the verse into short and meaningful phrases. Learn to quote the first phrase word for word. Then build on it by learning the second phrase. Continue until you can quote the entire verse word for word.
5. **Repeat the verse to another person and ask him to check your accuracy.**
6. **Regularly review the memorized verse.** During the first week carry the card in your pocket or purse. Pull it out for review several times daily during waiting periods—for example, when riding an elevator, riding to work, or taking a coffee or lunch break. Review the verse at least daily for the first six weeks. Review weekly for the next six weeks and monthly thereafter.

RESPONDING TO GOD'S ACTIVITY IN A GROUP

One of the lessons you need to learn from the Lord is how to respond to God's activity in a group experience. Normally, we have not been taught how to respond when God interrupts our group activities, plans, or programs. This is a lesson God can and will teach you. You can depend on Him. He cares far more for your group than you do. If He wants to work in the midst of that group to reveal Himself, He can and will enable you to respond appropriately. However, you must make some prior commitments in the way you function as a spiritual leader. You must give your plans and agenda to God. If He interrupts your group, cancel your agenda and see what God wants to do.

Henry and I were leading a conference together at the Glorieta Conference Center® formerly owned by Lifeway for 150 people. Small groups were just completing a sharing and prayer time, and I was about to turn the conference over to Henry. A woman stood and explained that one of the women in her group needed us to pray for her. The woman had been abused as a young child, and now her father was at home dying of cancer.

Henry and I have seen God bring dramatic emotional and spiritual healing to people in situations like that. I realized God wanted to do more than just share a prayer request with our group. I had to choose to pray briefly and turn the session over to Henry or to turn the session over to God. Henry and I had already agreed beforehand that if God ever interrupted us, we would cancel our agenda and give Him freedom to work. This is what we did.

I knew God had entrusted that woman's needs to this group, so I assumed He had also placed in that group the people who could best minister to her. I asked some women who could identify with her need to come and stand around her and pray with her. Eight or 10 women came to minister to her. I then gave an invitation for others to come for prayer if they had deep needs that only God could meet. People led by God came to minister to those who responded.

As God completed His work in a person's life, we gave her an opportunity to share with the group what God had done. Often God would use the testimony to invite someone with a similar problem to come to Him to be set free. For the rest of the hour, we watched as God used members in that group to minister to other members who had needs. People who had been in spiritual bondage for decades found freedom in Christ. Others experienced the comfort, healing, and peace that only God can give. Some, for the first time in their lives, experienced the love of a father—a Heavenly Father. Those whom God used in ministry to others experienced Him working through them in dramatic ways they had never experienced. We learned more about God that hour through experience than we could have learned in a week of lectures.

Here are some suggestions for responding to God's activity in your group.

1. Place your absolute trust in God to guide you when He wants to work in your group setting.

2. Decide beforehand that you will cancel your agenda and give God freedom to move anytime He shows you that He wants to do a special work. As you will learn as you study this course, there are some things only God can do. When you see Him at work in your group, that is your invitation to join Him.

3. Watch for things like tears of joy or conviction, emotional or spiritual brokenness, the thrill of a newfound insight, or a need for prayer in response to a need. These things are sometimes seen only in a facial expression. Determine whether you need to talk to the person now with the group or privately. You must depend on the Holy Spirit for such guidance. Be gentle and don't force responses.

4. Respond by asking a probing question like one of these: *Is something happening in your life that you would share with us? How may we pray for you? Would you share with us what God is doing in your life? What can we do to help you?*

5. If the person responds by sharing, then provide ministry based on the need. If he does not seem ready to respond, do not push or pressure him. Give God time to work in his life.

6. Invite members of the group to share in ministry to one another. This may be to pray, to comfort, to counsel privately, or to rejoice with the person. When you do not feel equipped to deal with a problem that surfaces, ask the group if one of them feels led to help. You will be amazed at how God works to provide just the right person to provide the needed ministry. If ministry outside the session seems appropriate, make those arrangements following the session.

7. Give people the opportunity to testify to what God is doing. This is a very critical point. Often God may use the testimony of one person to help another person with an identical problem or challenge. This is also one of the best ways for people to experience God—by hearing a testimony of His wonderful work in the life of another person. Do not hide God's glory from His people.

8. When you do not sense a clear direction about what to do next, ask the group. I have occasionally said, "I do not have a clear sense of what we need to do next. Does anyone have a sense of what God would want us to do?" Every time I have asked that, someone immediately responded with a direction that we all agreed was right.

I cannot identify all you may need to do. I cannot give you directions for handling every situation. But I can speak from experience: if God wants to work in the midst of a group, He can and will give the guidance needed for that time. Your job is to learn to recognize His voice and then do everything you sense He wants you to do. At the same time, trust Him to work through His body—the church. He has placed members in your group and gifted them to build up the body of Christ. Acknowledge and use all of the resources God has given to your group.

ADDITIONAL RESOURCES

The following leader tools, resources, and worksheets are available for download at lifeway.com/egleader.

Leader Tools:
- Introductory_Worksheets.pdf
- Scripture_Meditations.pdf
- EG_Evaluation.pdf
- Memorize_Scripture.pdf
- 7_Realities_Poster.pdf
- Bible_Prayer_Poster.pdf
- Unit_Posters.pdf

Tools to host an Experiencing God Weekend:
- Weekend_Manual.pdf
- Adult_Teaching_Plans.pdf
- Prayer_Guide.pdf
- PowerPoint_Slides
- Adult_Participant.pdf
- Children_Teaching_Plan.pdf
- Children_Workbook.pdf

NOTES

INTRODUCING
Experiencing God

BEFORE THE SESSION

❑ 1. Prepare yourself spiritually through a season of prayer for the upcoming study. Ask God to draw the people He wants to be involved in this study to the introductory session.

❑ 2. Read "During the Session." Adapt or develop the activities in a way that will best help your group understand the overview of the content and make a commitment to participate.

❑ 3. Decide on the amount of time to allow for each activity. Write a time in the margin to indicate when each activity should begin.

❑ 4. Gather the following items and any other items you need for activities you may have developed on your own.
   - One copy for each person of worksheets 1 and 2 (LG pp. 61–62)
   - The "Seven Realities" poster
   - The "Memorizing Scripture" poster
   - An index card for each person to use when registering for the study
   - *Optional:* A copy of "Scriptures for Meditation" (file *Scripture_Meditations.pdf* available for download at lifeway.com/egleader) for each member

❑ 5. If you have already prepared the unit posters (LG p. 9), display one from each unit on a focal wall to create interest.

❑ 6. *Optional:* Select a hymn, chorus, or recorded song for use during the group time. Arrange for accompaniment or bring an audio player

❑ 7. Read the description of learning activities in "During the Session" and identify the sections of content in the member book that you will explain in the session. Study those sections of material. If you want help, enlist one or more persons to help you explain various sections. For instance, you might want to get someone else to explain how Moses' life illustrates the seven realities of experiencing God.

❑ 8. If you have not completed all the preparations in "Leading a Small group Study of *Experiencing God*" (LG pp. 5–13), do so before the introductory session.

❑ 9. Enlist some help and provide light refreshments for the break.

DURING THE SESSION

Arrival Activity—5 minutes

1. Greet prospective members. Give each person a copy of worksheet 1 and ask participants to complete the activity while others are coming in.

2. Open with prayer (small group). Pray that God will use this session to give insight into His ways of revealing His will to persons and that He will guide each person present to respond to Him in making a decision about whether to study *Experiencing God.*

SESSION LEARNING OBJECTIVES

This session will help members—
- understand the approach of the study and how it will help members develop a deeper relationship with God;
- understand the commitments required to complete this course;
- demonstrate a commitment to complete individual study and group-session requirements for this course.

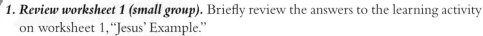

Course Overview—25–35 minutes

1. Review worksheet 1 (small group). Briefly review the answers to the learning activity on worksheet 1, "Jesus' Example."

2. Seven realities (small group). Distribute worksheet 2. Ask participants to read the seven statements and circle a key word or phrase in each. Using the explanation and Scriptures on pages 23–26 as background and the "Seven Realities" poster, briefly explain how Moses' experience with God illustrates how God works through people.

3. Experience God (small group). Explain how we come to know God by experience (p. 70). Describe Abraham's experience in Genesis 22:1-18 as an example of how a person comes to know God by experience. Give an example from your own experience. Then ask for a volunteer or two to briefly describe a time when they came to know God by experience.

4. Course overview (small group). Share with the group your reasons for leading this course. Then read the list of unit titles on the contents page (p. 3). Explain that this is not just a course. It is not a method or seven easy steps to knowing God's will. The course is designed to help members develop a relationship in which they clearly hear when God is speaking, recognize where He is working, join Him in His work, and experience Him working through them to accomplish His purposes.

Course Commitments—10 minutes

1. Elements in course (small group). Use the information on pages 9–10 to explain the requirements for individual study and participation in small group sessions. Emphasize that participants will be expected to spend about 30 minutes a day for five days each week to complete individual-study assignments.

2. Group covenant (small group). Read the text of the *Experiencing God* Group Covenant (p. 270) that members will be asked to sign if they decide to study the course.

3. Time and place (small group). Announce when groups will meet to study *Experiencing God.*

4. Questions and answers (small group). Answer any questions members have about the course.

Decision Time—5 minutes

1. Prayer (small group). Close the prayer time by asking God to clearly guide all present throughout the time together studying this course.

2. Enrollment time. Distribute index cards and ask members to write their names on the cards and to indicate one of the following: (1) Enroll me for the current study. (2) Notify me the next time the course is offered. (3) Please consider offering this study at another time (please specify day and time). (4) I'm unable to participate at this time.

Singing/Special Music—5 minutes

Optional special music (small group). Sing a familiar hymn or choruses or play a recorded song that relates to one of the subjects of this study. If you have selected a theme song for the study, sing it now.

Break—10 minutes

Explain that in the following hour you will distribute materials and will give specific instructions to those who plan to participate in the upcoming study. Invite everyone to enjoy refreshments.

Getting Ready for Next Week—30 minutes

1. Distribute materials (small group). Collect fees and give each person the following.

- *Experiencing God: Knowing and Doing the Will of God*
- Spiritual-journal notebook
- A copy of "Scriptures for Meditation" (optional file available for download at lifeway.com/egleader)

2. Explain individual-study requirements. Using unit 1 as an example, walk members through the process they will follow to complete each unit of study.

- Point out the verse of Scripture to memorize on page 6. Use the "Memorizing Scripture" poster you prepared to give suggestions on memorizing Scripture. Call attention to the Scripture-memory cards at the back of the member book. Explain that members can cut the cards apart and keep them in a pocket or purse for regular review.
- Point out pages 8–10 and ask members to review the information (you have covered most of it in this session) as they begin the study.
- Explain that content is divided into five daily assignments. Encourage members to study only one day at a time so they will have time to cultivate intimacy with God on a daily basis.
- Explain the interaction between the content and the learning activities. For an example ask members to turn to page 11 and complete activity 5.
- Explain that units 1 and 2 give a broad overview of the way God works in the lives of people. Units 3–9 go into greater detail on each of the seven realities of experiencing God. Units 10 and 11 focus on the church and the larger body of Christ called the Kingdom. Unit 12 helps members apply these truths to their daily lives. Repetition of writing and stating the seven realities will be used throughout the course to help members remember these biblical truths.
- Ask members to turn to page 13 and notice the review at the end of the day. Mention that this daily activity is designed for them to listen to what God may want to say to them. Encourage them to complete this activity daily. Mention that they may want to keep a running summary in their spiritual journal.

3. Explain the spiritual journal. Direct members to the instructions in "Keeping a Spiritual Journal" (p. 271). Point out the kinds of information they will want to record in their journals and how they may want to divide the notebook into categories. Ask members to bring their journals, Bibles, and workbooks to each group session because they will be used each week.

Covenant Making—10 minutes

1. Prepare the covenant (small group). Ask members to turn to page 270. Read again the covenant agreements. Give members an opportunity to discuss any changes or additions they want to make. Seek full agreement on the covenant. Then ask members to make the changes agreed to on their copies. Ask them to place their names on the blank line at the top.

2. Pray about keeping the covenant (small group). Pray that God will draw this group into a deeper fellowship with Him and with one another during the coming weeks. Ask each person to pray a sentence prayer asking for God's strength and guidance to complete the course and keep this covenant with the other group members.

3. Sign the covenant (small group). Ask individuals to sign their own covenants and then to sign the covenant of each group member. Be sensitive to any members who may not be ready to fully enter the covenant. Indicate that they will have an opportunity to do so when they are ready.

Closure—5 minutes
Express your own feelings about studying together with this group. Then ask a member to lead the group in a prayer of commitment to God and to one another for the duration of this course.

AFTER THE SESSION

1. Add to your spiritual journal the names of group members and ways you can pray for each one. Do you sense a need to pray intently for any person in particular? If so, record concerns you need to pray about for that person.
2. Ask yourself the following questions and write notes on the lines provided, in the margin, or in your journal.
    • What spiritual or mental preparation do I need to make for the next session that may have been lacking this week? _____
    _____
    _____

    • How well did I begin and end on time? _____
    _____
    _____

3. Save all posters for use in later sessions or for future introductory sessions.
4. Give information from the enrollment cards to the appropriate person in your church. Encourage your discipleship-training director to make every possible effort to provide a group study for those who request a different time.
5. If you had more than 10 people in your group, enlist an additional leader and divide the group prior to next week.
6. If you need additional resources, secure them. If you do not have enough member books, order additional copies from one of the sources listed in the margin on LG page 8.

GOD'S WILL AND YOUR LIFE

BEFORE THE SESSION

❑ 1. Complete all learning activities in unit 1 of the member book.

❑ 2. Pause and pray for God's guidance as you prepare for this week's group session. Pray for each member of your group. Ask God to help members be moldable throughout this course so that He can shape their lives into vessels that are useful to His kingdom work.

❑ 3. Read "During the Session." Select the activities that best suit the learning needs of your group. Adapt or develop other activities you sense will best help your group gain the greatest benefit from the unit of study.

❑ 4. Decide on the amount of time to allow for each activity. Write a time (for instance, write 6:20 beside "Sharing Time") in the margin to indicate when each activity should begin. These times should help you stay on schedule through the session. Always be prepared to change your plans if the Holy Spirit leads you and the group in another direction.

❑ 5. Arrange the chairs in a circle.

❑ 6. Prepare seven Scripture-reference slips by writing each of the following Scripture references on a separate card or slip of paper: John 7:16; John 8:28-29; John 10:37-38; John 12:49-50; John 14:10; John 17:8; Acts 2:22.

❑ 7. Gather the following items and any other items you need for activities you may have developed on your own.
  • Index cards and pencils for members to provide contact information
  • Name tags and markers
  • The "Memorizing Scripture" poster from the introductory session
  • The "Seven Realities" poster from the introductory session

❑ 8. Display on a focal wall the unit posters you have prepared (LG p. 9).

❑ 9. *Optional:* Select a hymn, chorus, or recorded song for use during the group time.

❑ 10. Prepare a one-minute preview of unit 2.

❑ 11. If you are using the video teaching messages, do the following.
  • Secure and set up the equipment necessary for viewing.
  • Preview the session 1 video teaching session (18:47 min.) and list one or two key ideas or questions you think will be of special interest to your group members. Use these ideas to introduce the video message.
  • Think through your own response to the discussion question in "During the Session."

SESSION LEARNING OBJECTIVES

This session will help members—
• recall the seven realities of experiencing God;
• recognize Jesus' example for doing God's will;
• identify ways they can pray for fellow members;
• identify and express God's activity in their lives.

NOTE: Each time you divide the small group into pairs or quads, give verbal instructions to everyone. If you think they need more help, write the instructions on a dry-erase board or on newsprint.

DURING THE SESSION

Arrival Activity—5 minutes

1. Greet members as they arrive. Give them an information card and ask for their name and contact information (phone and e-mail). Provide name tags. Ask them to complete the unit review on page 29 while others are coming in.

2. Prepare. As some finish writing, give to different members the seven Scripture-reference slips you prepared. Ask each one to find the Scripture and mark it for reading later in the session.

3. Get acquainted. Ask members to share their responses to the "Get Acquainted" statements in the margin on page 29.

4. Open with prayer (small group). After members have had time to share, thank God for bringing this group of people together. Acknowledge God's presence in your midst and ask the Holy Spirit to be your Teacher during the session. Ask Him to begin bonding your lives together in Christian love and unity during the sessions of this study.

Unit Review—15 minutes

1. Review (small group). Ask members to turn to the unit review on page 29. Tell members they will be asked to complete a simple review like this for each unit. Explain that the activities are simply intended for review. Individuals will check their own answers. In some cases the review questions will be part of the sharing time.

2. Seven realities (small group). Display the poster with the seven-realities diagram. Mention the key words *(God's work)* for the first reality and ask someone to state the first reality in her own words. Do the same for each of the other six realities.

3. Jesus' example (small group). Ask one member to read the summary of Jesus' example for following the will of His Father (p. 16). Then call for the seven Scriptures to be read by the persons enlisted earlier in the session. Suggest that members may want to mark these verses in their Bibles or record the references in their member books on page 16. Ask and then discuss the answers to these questions:

   a. Who was doing the work we see in the life of Jesus? Was Jesus doing His own work, or was God the Father doing His work through Jesus?

   b. Whose words did Jesus speak—His own or His Father's?

4. Q & A (small group). Ask volunteers to answer the following.

   a. What are two things a servant must do to be used by God? (p. 17)

   b. Why do you think God likes to do His work through ordinary people?
   (p. 28 and 1 Cor. 1:26-31)

Sharing Time—30 minutes

1. Scripture memory (pairs). Ask members to quote John 15:5 to each other. If some are having trouble, give words of encouragement and review the suggestions for memorizing Scripture (LG p. 11). Ask each person to share with his or her partner what God may have said to him or her through this week's memory verse.

2. Most meaningful (quads). Ask members to review their five most meaningful statements or Scriptures for the unit (pp. 13, 16, 20, 24, and 28) and identify the one statement or Scripture that was the most meaningful of these five. Ask members to (a) read their most meaningful statements or Scriptures, (b) tell why they were meaningful, and (c) share how they responded to God in prayer.

Get Acquainted

1. My name is …
2. My immediate family includes …
3. The thing I liked best about my hometown was …
4. Something interesting you might not know about me is …
5. I chose to study this course on knowing and doing the will of God because …

Jesus' Example

- John 7:16
- John 8:28-29
- John 10:37-38
- John 12:49-50
- John 14:10
- John 17:8
- Acts 2:22

3. *Declare the wonderful works of the Lord (small group).* Allow time for testimonies. Say: *If God has done something special in or through your life this week, please share what He has done so we can praise the Lord together.*

4. *Focus on God (small group).* Ask:
   a. *What have you come to know about God, His purposes, or His ways this week?*
   b. *What do you sense God wants you to do in response to Him?*

Prayer Time—15 minutes

1. *Share requests and pray (quads).* (Be sure to use smaller groups of about four so members will have time to pray for each person.) Ask each person to share one way the others can pray for him or her. Suggest that the group pray for one member at a time by allowing several people to pray for that member. Then allow the small group to pray for a second member. Ask the group to continue praying until everyone has been prayed for. Tell the groups that a person does not have to pray aloud unless he or she wants to. As time goes by, most members will feel comfortable praying in small groups.

2. *Record prayer requests (small group).* As groups finish praying, suggest: *Turn to the prayer section of your journal and record prayer requests or ways God led you to pray for individuals in your small group. Remember these persons in your prayer times this next week.*

Singing/Special Music—5 minutes

Optional special music (small group). Sing a hymn or chorus or play a recorded song that relates to servanthood or following Jesus' example, such as "Footsteps of Jesus" or "Wherever He Leads I'll Go." If you have chosen a theme song for your group, practice learning and singing it now.

Video Teaching Viewing and Discussion—45 minutes

1. *View the video teaching for session 1 (small group).* Invite members to turn to the viewer guide on page 29 and view session 1.

2. *Discuss the message (small group).* Ask and discuss the following questions or use your own.
   a. *What are some of the important factors in knowing and doing the will of God?*
   b. *What one truth did you hear that was most contrary to human reasoning?*

Closure—5 minutes

1. *Wait on the Lord (small group).* Review any questions or concerns that may have come up during the session. Ask the group to pray for these concerns and seek answers during the coming week.

2. *Preview unit 2 (small group).* Ask members to pay special attention to the difference between self-centered and God-centered living as they study unit 2 this week.

3. *Pray (small group).* Stand and join hands. Ask volunteers to pray one-sentence prayers of personal commitment to God for the duration of this course. Explain that you will *not* pray around the circle and that anyone who does not want to pray aloud has permission to pass by simply not praying.

If your group had more than 8 to 10 members, plan to divide it. Enlist another leader (preferably from those already in the group). If you cannot enlist another leader, consider dividing into two groups and meeting at different times during the week. If you must have more than 10 members in your group, be sure to divide into smaller groups for sharing, discussion, and prayer in the coming weeks.

AFTER THE SESSION

Use the standard guide on LG page 63 to evaluate the session.

SESSION 2

LOOKING TO GOD

SESSION LEARNING OBJECTIVES

This session will help members—

• state in their own words the seven realities of experiencing God;

• define the difference between self-centered and God-centered living and give one biblical example of each;

• yield their wills to the lordship of Christ.

BEFORE THE SESSION

❑ 1. Complete all learning activities in unit 2 of the member book.

❑ 2. Pray now for God's guidance as you prepare for this group session. Pray specifically for each member of your group.

❑ 3. Read "During the Session." Select the activities that best suit the learning needs of your group. Adapt or develop other activities you sense will best help your group gain the greatest benefit from the unit of study.

❑ 4. Decide on the amount of time to allow for each activity. Write a time in the margin to indicate when each activity should begin. Always be prepared to change your plans if the Holy Spirit leads you and the group in another direction.

❑ 5. Gather the "Seven Realities" poster and any other items you need for activities you may have developed on your own. Provide additional name tags if members have not adequately learned the names of others in the group.

❑ 6. Make sure each member has a member book and a spiritual journal. If you know of a member who does not have both, try to get them to the member for use before the next group session. Make sure any new members have both resources and understand the need to complete the learning activities in the unit prior to the group session.

❑ 7. Remove the unit posters from the previous session and save them for use in a future study of *Experiencing God*. Display the posters you have prepared for unit 2 (LG p. 9).

❑ 8. Prepare a one-minute preview of unit 3.

❑ 9. If you are using the video teaching sessions, do the following.

  • Secure and set up the equipment necessary for viewing.

  • Preview the session 2 video teaching (16:37 min.) and list one or two key ideas or questions you think will be of special interest to your group members. Use these ideas to introduce this session's teaching.

  • Think through your own response to the video teaching discussion questions in "During the Session." Think about how you will respond after "Prayer Time" if people have been deeply touched by the Lord.

DURING THE SESSION

Arrival Activity—5 minutes

1. Greet members as they arrive. Ask them to complete the unit review on page 49 while others are coming in. Make sure they have completed the learning activities that will be discussed in "Sharing Time."

2. Open with prayer (small group). Ask a volunteer to open the session with a prayer. Suggest that all members pray silently for God to guide them to more God-centered living.

Unit Review—20 minutes

1. Review (small group). Review and discuss, if needed, the answers to the true/false and fill-in-the-blank questions in the unit review. Remind members that they will have a simple activity like this each week to begin a review of the unit's content. Encourage members to complete all the learning activities in a unit prior to the group sessions so they can actively participate in the discussion-and-sharing times.

2. Seven realities (small group). Using the "Seven Realities" poster, review the seven realities of experiencing God. See if members can state (in their own words) the seven realities without hints. If they have trouble, give them the key words as hints.

3. Q & A (small group). As time permits, ask volunteers to answer the following.

   a. What is the difference between self-centered and God-centered living (p. 32)?

   b. How is King Asa an example of both kinds of living (activity 2 [3a–b], p. 33)?

   c. How did George Müller seek God's directions for his life (pp. 39–41)?

   d. How did God speak in the Old Testament? During the life of Jesus (activity 1, p. 42)?

   e. How does God speak in our day (activity 3, p. 43)?

   f. What is the key to knowing God's voice (activities 4 and 5, p. 44)?

4. Poster discussion (small group). Focus attention on the statements on the unit posters you have displayed. Read each statement and ask members to comment on what that statement means to them. Ask what adjustments may be needed in their lives to relate correctly to God.

Sharing Time—30 minutes

1. Scripture memory (pairs). Ask members to quote Psalm 20:7 to each other and share what God may have said to them through this week's memory verse.

2. Written responses (quads). Ask members to share and discuss with one another their responses to the "Sharing Time" topics on page 49:

   • The questions about God's judgment, activity 5, page 37

   • The questions on lordship and character building, activity 4, pages 47–48

   • One of the most meaningful statements or Scriptures from this unit's lessons and your prayer response to God. Choose one from pages 34, 38, 41, 45, and 48.

3. Focus on God (pairs). Ask:

   a. What have you come to know about God, His purposes, or His ways this week?

   b. What do you sense God wants you to do in response to this knowledge of Him?

4. Declare the wonderful works of the Lord (small group). Allow time for testimonies. Say: *If God has done something special in or through your life this week, please share what God has done so we can praise the Lord together.*

Video teaching Viewing and Discussion—45 minutes

1. *View the video teaching for session 2 (small group).* Invite members to turn to the viewer guide on page 49 and view session 2.

2. *Discuss the message and testimony (small group).* Ask and discuss the following questions or use your own.

    a. *What are some ways Mike's story about receiving a mysterious package help us understand why it's important for us to see God as the center of our lives?*

    b. *What are some of the differences between being God-centered and being human-centered?*

    c. *What is the most encouraging description of God or statement about His ways you heard in this session?*

Prayer Time—15 minutes

1. *Record prayer requests (small group).* Ask members to turn to the prayer section of their journals and prepare to record the prayer requests that are shared in the following activity.

2. *Share requests and pray (small group).* Ask each person to give the group a one-sentence prayer request. The request could relate to the individual, his family, his church, his work, a friend, or a relative. Suggest that some requests may focus on spiritual concerns that have arisen as a result of this study. After each person has shared a request, ask members to pray conversationally for the needs expressed by fellow group members.

Closure—5 minutes

1. *Wait on the Lord (small group).* Review any questions or concerns that may have come up during the session. Ask the group to pray for these concerns and seek answers to questions during the coming week.

2. *Preview unit 3 (small group).* Ask members to pay special attention to the worship assignment on day 3 (activity 2, p. 60) and to allot ample time for their walk with God.

3. *Pray (small group).* Stand in a circle and join hands. Call on one member to express a prayer of commitment that the group will always look only to God for directions in His kingdom's work.

AFTER THE SESSION

Use the standard guide on LG page 63 to evaluate the session.

GOD PURSUES A LOVE RELATIONSHIP

BEFORE THE SESSION

❏ 1. Complete all learning activities in unit 3 of the member book.

❏ 2. Pray now for God's guidance as you prepare for this group session. Pray specifically for each member of your group.

❏ 3. Read "During the Session." Select the activities that best suit the learning needs of your group. Adapt or develop other activities you sense will best help your group gain the greatest benefit from the unit of study.

❏ 4. Decide on the amount of time to allow for each activity. Write a time in the margin to indicate when each activity should begin. Always be prepared to change plans if the Holy Spirit leads you and the group in another direction.

❏ 5. Gather the "Seven Realities" poster and any other items you need for activities you may have developed on your own.

❏ 6. Remove the unit posters from the previous session and save them for future use. Display the posters you have prepared for unit 3 (LG p. 9).

❏ 7. *Optional:* Select a hymn, chorus, or recorded song for use during the large group time.

❏ 8. Prepare a one-minute preview of unit 4.

❏ 9. If you are using the video teaching sessions, do the following.
- Secure and set up the equipment necessary for viewing.
- Preview the session 3 video teaching (18:28 min.) and list one or two key ideas or questions you think will be of special interest to your group members. Use these ideas to introduce the teaching.
- Think about your response to the discussion questions in "During the Session." Think about how you will respond after "Prayer Time" if people have been deeply touched by the Lord.

DURING THE SESSION

Arrival Activity—5 minutes

1. *Greet members as they arrive.* Ask them to complete the unit review on page 67 while others are coming in and to make sure they have completed the learning activities that will be discussed in "Sharing Time."

2. *Open with prayer.* Ask volunteers to express statements of praise, thanksgiving, and adoration to God for who He is and what He has done. Close with a prayer asking for God's guidance during the session.

Unit Review—15 minutes

1. *Review (small group).* Discuss the answers to the first two questions in the unit review. Ask questions like these:
- *What are you becoming in Christ?*
- *How should that influence your life today?*
- *How did Paul deal with his past (activity 6, p. 57)?*

SESSION LEARNING OBJECTIVES

This session will help members—
- quote the first two statements of the realities of experiencing God;
- identify biblical examples of a love relationship with God that is real, personal, and practical;
- identify and verbalize times in their lives when they experienced God as real, personal, and practical.

• *Can a human ever take the initiative in establishing a love relationship with God? Why or why not?* (No, whenever a person seeks God, he does so because God is drawing him. No one seeks God on his own initiative. See day 4, page 61.)

2. *Seven realities (pairs).* Ask members to form pairs and state to their partners the first two realities of experiencing God. If they need hints, give them the key words *God's work* and *relationship.*

3. *Q & A (small group).* As time permits, ask volunteers to answer the following:
   a. *In what ways God has demonstrated His love for us (activity 6b, p. 54)?*
   b. *How can we show our love for God (activity 6c, p. 54)?*
   c. *What are some biblical examples in which a relationship with God was real, personal, and practical (activity 1, p. 64)?*

4. *Poster discussion (small group).* Focus attention on the statements on the unit posters you have displayed. Read each statement and ask members to comment on what that statement means to them. Ask what adjustments may be needed in their lives to relate correctly to God.

Sharing Time—30 minutes

1. *Scripture memory (pairs).* Ask members to quote Matthew 22:37-38 to each other and share what God may have said to them through this memory verse.

2. *Written responses (quads).* Ask members to turn in their books to the following learning activities and share responses with one another. Topics are listed in the "Sharing Time" box with the review.
   • Things in which you are investing your life, time, and resources and the adjustments God wants you to make (activities 7 and 8, pp. 58–59).
   • Reasons you know God loves you (activity 3, p. 62).
   • An experience when God was real, personal, and practical in his relationship with you (activity 2, p. 65).
   • One of the most meaningful statements or Scriptures from this unit's lessons and your prayer response to God. Choose one from pages 55, 59, 63, and 66.

3. *Focus on God (quads).* Ask:
   a. *What have you come to know about God, His purposes, or His ways this week?*
   b. *What do you sense God wants you to do in response to this knowledge of Him?*

4. *Walk with God (small group).* Give volunteers an opportunity to share about their experiences walking with God (activity 2, p. 60). Share your own experience as a model for the others.

5. *Testimonies (small group).* Give members an opportunity to share what God may have been doing in their lives during this week and in this session. However, do not force people to share. As a leader, be very sensitive to what may be happening during this time. If God reveals to you that He is moving deeply in a person's life, this is a time to make major adjustments. If one or more individuals are deeply moved by this time of prayer and testimony, spend extra time with the ones deeply touched by the Lord. Enlist the help of other group members to pray with and for these individuals. Stay with them until they sense peace about this encounter with God.

6. *Declare the wonderful works of the Lord (small group).* Allow time for testimonies. Say: *If God has done something special in or through your life this week, please share what God has done so we can praise the Lord together.*

Prayer Time—15 minutes

1. Pray Psalm 103 (small group). Ask members to turn in their Bibles to Psalm 103. As an expression of gratitude to God for His love, join in a group reading of this psalm. Remind members that blessing the Lord through this reading can be a form of worship and prayer. Suggest that one member read a verse; then the person to his left reads the second verse. Continue reading one verse at a time until you have completed reading the entire psalm.

2. Expressing your love to God (quads). Ask members to spend the next few minutes in quads expressing their love to God in prayer. This may include thanksgiving, praise, or statements of commitment.

Singing/Special Music—5 minutes

Optional special music (small group). Sing a hymn or chorus or play a recorded song that relates to love for God and God's love for you. You might select a song like "Jesus Paid It All," "In the Garden," "Love Lifted Me," or "More than Wonderful." If time permits, ask for any special requests and sing one or two.

Video Teaching Viewing and Discussion—45 minutes

1. View the Video teaching for session 3 (small group). Invite members to turn to the viewer guide on page 67 and view session 3.

2. Discuss the message and testimony (small group). Ask and discuss the following questions or use your own.

  a. What can Richard's story about the young woman struggling with depression and suicidal thoughts teach us about the way God lovingly pursues His children?

  b. What does the biblical story of the prophet Hosea teach us about God's pursuing love?

  c. What are some ways earthly fathers can distort the idea of a father's love?
   And what has God said and done to prove that His perfect love is different?

3. Prayer response (individual). Ask members to kneel at their chairs (if they are able) and spend a few minutes responding to God privately. Suggest that they may want to ask God for forgiveness, healing of emotional scars from the past, or help in dealing with another issue that God brings to mind.

Closure—5 minutes

1. Wait on the Lord (small group). Review any questions or concerns that may have come up during the session. Ask the group to pray for these concerns and seek answers to questions during the coming week.

2. Preview unit 4 (small group). Ask members to pay special attention to how God reveals His invitation for them to join Him in His work.

3. Pray (quads). Ask members to close the session by thanking God and praying for the other three members in their quad. Suggest that members leave quietly as the others finish praying.

AFTER THE SESSION

Use the standard guide on LG page 63 to evaluate the session.

SESSION 4

LOVE AND GOD'S INVITATION

SESSION LEARNING OBJECTIVES

This session will help members—

- match three statements about the nature of God with important implications for the life of a believer;
- describe the way someone comes to know God personally and intimately;
- recognize the initiative and activity of God around their lives;
- demonstrate worship of God through prayers and testimonies offered in His name.

BEFORE THE SESSION

❏ 1. Complete all learning activities in unit 4 of the member book.
❏ 2. Pray now for God's guidance as you prepare for this group session. Pray specifically for each member of your group.
❏ 3. Read "During the Session." Select the activities that best suit the learning needs of your group. Adapt or develop other activities you sense will best help your group gain the greatest benefit from the unit of study.
❏ 4. Decide on the amount of time to allow for each activity. Write a time in the margin to indicate when each activity should begin. Always be prepared to change your plans if the Holy Spirit leads you and the group in another direction.
❏ 5. Gather the "Seven Realities" poster and any other items you need for activities you may have developed on your own.
❏ 6. Remove the unit posters from the previous session and save them for future use. Display the posters you have prepared for unit 4 (LG p. 9).
❏ 7. *Optional:* Select a hymn, chorus, or recorded song for use during the large group time.
❏ 8. Prepare a one-minute preview of unit 5.
❏ 9. If you are using the video teaching sessions, do the following.
  • Secure and set up the equipment necessary for viewing.
  • Preview the session 4 video teaching (18:16 min.) and list one or two key ideas or questions you think will be of special interest to your group members. Use these ideas to introduce the video teaching.
  • Think about your own response to the video teaching discussion questions in "During the Session."
❏ 10. As a review of important information, reread LG pages 5–13. Pay special attention to the suggestions for responding to God's activity in a group. Continue to review these pages from time to time to keep them fresh on your mind.

DURING THE SESSION

Arrival Activity—5 minutes
1. *Greet members as they arrive.* Ask them to complete the unit review on page 87 while others are coming in and to make sure they have completed the learning activities that will be discussed in "Sharing Time."
2. *Open with prayer (small group).* Ask members to think of one name by which they have come to know God through experience. Ask each one to pray a sentence prayer of thanksgiving for God's revealing Himself as a personal and living God.

Unit Review—15 minutes
1. *Review (small group).* Review and discuss, if needed, the answers to the activities in the review. Ask members how they felt when they studied the three truths about God described in the matching activity of the review.
2. *Q & A (small group).* As time permits, ask volunteers to answer the following.
   a. *How do you come to know God personally and intimately (p. 72)?*
   b. *What are some of the many ways we can worship God through His names (p. 74)?*
   c. *What is the purpose of God's commands (p. 77)?*
   d. *How did Jesus know the will of His Father (p. 79)?*
   e. *What are two factors important to your recognizing God's activity around you (p. 80)?*
   f. *What are some actions you can take to see whether God is at work in a situation (p. 84)?*
   g. *When does God speak (p. 85)?*
   h. *When God takes the initiative to accomplish something through an individual or a church, what does He guarantee (p. 86)?*
3. *Poster discussion (small group).* Focus attention on the statements on the unit posters you have displayed. Read each statement and ask members to comment on what that statement means to them. Ask what adjustments may be needed in their lives to relate correctly to God.
4. *Seven realities (pairs).* Ask partners to state to each other the first three realities of experiencing God.

Sharing Time—30 minutes
1. *Scripture memory (quads).* Ask members to quote John 14:21 to one another and share what God may have said to them through this week's memory verse.
2. *Declare the wonderful works of the Lord (small group).* Allow time for testimonies. Say: *If God has done something special in or through your life this week, please share what God has done so we can praise the Lord together.*
3. *Focus on God (small group).* Ask:
   a. *What have you come to know about God, His purposes, or His ways this week?*
   b. *What do you sense God wants you to do in response to this knowledge of Him?*
4. *Written responses (small group).* Ask members to turn in their books to the following learning activities and share responses with one another. Topics are listed in the "Sharing Time" box with the review.
   • An event through which you have come to know God by experience and the name that describes Him (p. 71)
5. *Move to quads.* Continue sharing your responses to the following:
   • What you thought, felt, or experienced during your time of worship on day 2 (p. 74)
   • Ideas you may have for recognizing God's activity around you (p. 85)
   • One of the most meaningful statements or Scriptures from this unit's lessons and your prayer response to God. Choose one from pages 72, 77, 81, and 86.

Prayer Time—15 minutes

1. *Share requests and pray (quads).* Ask members to look at the names of God on pages 268–69 and identify one by which they sense a need to know God. Then ask them to share with the others the name and why they sense a need to know God that way. For instance, one person might say, "My parents divorced when I was young, and I never got to know my father. I sense a deep need to know God as the loving Heavenly Father." After all members have shared their sense of need, encourage quads to pray specifically for those in their group.

2. *Record prayer requests (small group).* As groups finish praying, suggest: *Turn to the prayer section of your journal and record prayer requests or ways God led you to pray for individuals in your group.*

Singing/Special Music—5 minutes

Optional special music (small group). Sing a hymn or chorus or play a recorded song that relates to God's names, such as "His Name Is Wonderful," "How Majestic Is Your Name," "Jesus Is the Sweetest Name I Know," or "We Will Glorify." For special music you might play a recording of "El Shaddai" or a contemporary song.

Video Teaching Viewing and Discussion—45 minutes

1. *View the video teaching for session 4 (small group).* Invite members to turn to the viewer guide on page 87 and view session 4.

2. *Discuss the message and testimony (small group).* Ask and discuss the following questions or use your own.

   a. *How should we view and respond to God's invitation to join Him in His activity if we are to live impactful Christian lives?*

   b. *What statement or Scripture did you hear that stirred a spirit of hope or conviction, and how do you need to respond to the Lord?*

   c. *How would you respond to Mike's question in this session: When you pray, do you stop and watch what God does after you pray? What changes when we stop and watch?*

Closure—5 minutes

1. *Wait on the Lord (small group).* Review any questions or concerns that may have come up during the session. Ask the group to pray for these concerns and seek answers to questions during the coming week.

2. *Preview unit 5 (small group).* Ask members to pay special attention to how God speaks to them this week through the Bible and prayer.

3. *Pray (small group).* If your group would be responsive to a different expression of worship, suggest that they follow the psalmist's example and lift up their hands in His name. As members stand with eyes gazing toward heaven and hands lifted in His name, express a prayer of praise to God for His great love and a prayer of submission to His will and purposes.

AFTER THE SESSION

Use the standard guide on LG page 63 to evaluate the session.

GOD SPEAKS, PART 1

BEFORE THE SESSION

❑ 1. Complete all the learning activities in unit 5 of the member book. Be sure you have prepared your own spiritual inventory or list of spiritual markers.

❑ 2. Pray now for God's guidance as you prepare for this group session. Pray specifically for each member of your group.

❑ 3. Read "During the Session." Select the activities that best suit the learning needs of your group. Adapt or develop other activities you sense will best help your group gain the greatest benefit from the unit of study.

❑ 4. Decide on the amount of time to allow for each activity. Write a time in the margin to indicate when each activity should begin. Always be prepared to change your plans if the Holy Spirit leads you and the group in another direction.

❑ 5. Gather the "Seven Realities" poster and any other items you need for activities you may have developed on your own.

❑ 6. Prepare two diagram posters on poster board. Draw the diagram for the way God speaks through the Bible (p. 104) on one poster and the diagram for prayer (p. 108) on the other (or download print *Bible_Prayer_Poster.pdf* available for download at lifeway.com/egleader). Because you may use these posters for future groups of *Experiencing God*, you may want to laminate them to protect them.

❑ 7. Remove the unit posters from the previous session and save them for future use. Display the posters you have prepared for unit 5 (LG p. 9).

❑ 8. Prepare a one-minute preview of unit 6. Pay special attention to the activity for preparing a spiritual inventory on page 127 so you can warn members to allow time for it.

❑ 9. If you are using the video teaching sessions, do the following.
  • Secure and set up the equipment necessary for viewing.
  • Preview the session 5 video teaching (17:34 min.) and list one or two key ideas or questions you think will be of special interest to your group members. Use these ideas to introduce the video teaching.
  • Think about your own response to the video teaching discussion questions in "During the Session." Think about how you will respond after "Prayer Time" if people have been deeply touched by the Lord.

SESSION LEARNING OBJECTIVES

This session will help members—

• identify three of four important factors in the way God spoke in the Old Testament;

• identify the reasons God reveals Himself, His purposes, and His ways;

• explain how God speaks through the Bible and prayer;

• demonstrate concern for a partner by praying for his or her greatest spiritual challenge.

DURING THE SESSION

Arrival Activity—5 minutes

1. Greet members as they arrive. Ask them to complete the unit review on page 111 while others are coming in and to make sure they have completed the learning activities that will be discussed in "Sharing Time."

2. Open with prayer (small group). Ask one member to lead in prayer thanking God for revealing Himself, His purposes, and His ways.

Unit Review—15 minutes

1. Review (small group). Review and discuss, if needed, the answers to the first and last activities in the unit review.

2. Seven realities (small group). Ask one member to use the "Seven Realities" poster and review for the group the first four realities of experiencing God. If he needs help, prompt him by giving him the key word or words.

3. Bible and prayer diagrams (small group). Ask a member to use the "God Speaks Through the Bible" poster to explain how God speaks through the Bible. Discuss any questions members may have about the way God speaks through His Word. Then ask a different member to use the "God Speaks Through Prayer" poster to explain how God speaks through prayer. Discuss any questions members may have about the way God speaks through prayer.

4. Poster discussion (small group). Focus attention on the statements on the unit posters you have displayed. Read each statement and ask members to comment on what that statement means to them. Ask what adjustments may be needed in their lives to relate correctly to God.

5. Q & A (small group). As time permits, ask volunteers to answer the following.

a. What is the most important factor we learn from studying the ways God spoke in the Old Testament (p. 90)?

b. How did God speak in the Gospels (p. 94)?

c. What is the role of the Holy Spirit in prayer (pp. 108–9)?

Sharing Time—30 minutes

1. Written responses (quads). Ask members to turn in their books to the following learning activities and share responses with one another. Topics are listed in the "Sharing Time" box with the review.

- *What God has been saying in this course* (p. 96)
- *What God has said through the Bible* (p. 104)
- *What God has said through prayer* (p. 110)
- One of the most meaningful statements or Scriptures from this unit's lessons and your prayer response to God. Choose one from pages 94, 97, 102, 106, and 110.

2. Focus on God (small group). Ask:

a. What have you come to know about God, His purposes, or His ways this week?

b. What do you sense God wants you to do in response to this knowledge?

3. Declare the wonderful works of the Lord (small group). Allow time for testimonies. Say: *If God has done something special in or through your life this week, please share what God has done so we can praise the Lord together.*

4. Scripture memory (pairs). Ask members to quote John 8:47 to each other and share what God may have said to them through this week's memory verse.

Video Teaching Viewing and Discussion—45 minutes
1. *View the video teaching for session 5 (small group).* Invite members to turn to the viewer guide on page 111 and view session 5.
2. *Discuss the message and testimony (small group).* Ask and discuss the following questions or use your own.
   a. *How does Richard's story about learning to communicate with His wife as a newlywed teach us about our need to understand when God is speaking to us?*
   b. *How does God use the Scripture and prayer to speak to us?*
   c. *Thinking back to Richard's conversation with Mike at the end of the video teaching, what should we in those moments when it feels as though God is silent?*

Prayer Time—20 minutes
1. *Share requests and pray (pairs).* Ask members to share their greatest spiritual challenge (p. 96) with their partners. After one member shares her spiritual challenge, ask her partner to pray specifically for her. Then reverse roles and ask the other member to share his spiritual challenge. Then take time for his partner to pray for him.
2. *Record prayer requests (small group).* As pairs finish praying, suggest: *Turn to the prayer section of your journal and record the spiritual challenge of your partner so you can continue to pray for him or her.*

Closure—5 minutes
1. *Wait on the Lord (small group).* Review any questions or concerns that may have come up during the session. Ask the group to pray for these concerns and seek answers to questions during the coming week.
2. *Preview unit 6 (small group).* Ask members to pay special attention to the way God may use spiritual markers (day 4) to guide them in decision making. Tell them to allow time to prepare their lists of spiritual markers before the next group session.
3. *Pray (small group).* Join hands. Instead of giving a topic for prayer, suggest that members pray conversationally as the Holy Spirit prompts them.

AFTER THE SESSION

Use the standard guide on LG page 63 to evaluate the session.

SESSION 6

GOD SPEAKS, PART 2

SESSION LEARNING OBJECTIVES

This session will help members—

• write the first four realities of experiencing God in their own words;

• identify two possible reasons for silence from God when they pray;

• explain how to respond when faced with confusing circumstances;

• demonstrate an understanding of God's personal guidance in their lives by describing the spiritual markers in their lives.

BEFORE THE SESSION

❑ 1. Complete all the learning activities in unit 6 of the member book.

❑ 2. Pray now for God's guidance as you prepare for this group session. Pray specifically for each member of your group.

❑ 3. Read "During the Session." Select the activities that best suit the learning needs of your group. Adapt or develop other activities you sense will best help your group gain the greatest benefit from the unit of study.

❑ 4. Decide on the amount of time to allow for each activity. Write a time in the margin to indicate when each activity should begin. Always be prepared to change your plans if the Holy Spirit leads you and the group in another direction.

❑ 5. Gather the "Seven Realities" poster and any other items you need for activities you may have developed on your own.

❑ 6. Remove the unit posters from the previous session and save them for future use. Display the posters you have prepared for unit 6 (LG p. 9).

❑ 7. *Optional:* Select a hymn, chorus, or recorded song for use during the large group time.

❑ 8. Prepare a preview of unit 7 and be prepared to share the instructions listed in "During the Session" for this preview.

❑ 9. If you are using the video teaching, do the following.
  • Secure and set up the equipment necessary for viewing.
  • Preview the session 6 video teaching (19:17 min.) and list one or two key ideas or questions you think will be of special interest to your group members. Use these ideas to introduce the session's video teaching.

DURING THE SESSION

Arrival Activity—5 minutes

1. Greet members as they arrive. Ask them to complete the unit review on page 131 while others are coming in and to make sure they have completed the learning activities that will be discussed in "Sharing Time."

2. Open with prayer (small group). Lead in prayer and include a request that God speak and work through the members of this group to help one another better understand His will for their lives.

Unit Review—15 minutes

1. Seven realities (small group). Ask for a volunteer (different from the one who stated the four realities in the previous session) to use the "Seven Realities" poster and review the first four realities of experiencing God.

2. Poster discussion (small group). Focus attention on the statements on the unit posters you have displayed. Read each statement and ask members to comment on what that statement means to them. Ask what adjustments may be needed in their lives.

3. Q & A (small group). As time permits, ask volunteers to answer the following:

   a. What are two possible reasons for God's silence when you pray (p. 116)?

   b. What should a Christian do when faced with circumstances that are confusing (p. 120)?

   c. When do you really know the truth of a given situation (pp. 121–22)?

   d. How does a Christian come to understand his or her role in the body of Christ (pp. 128–30)?

Sharing Time—30 minutes

1. Spiritual markers (small group). Share some of your own spiritual markers (assigned on p. 127). Then ask volunteers to share some of the spiritual markers they have identified in their lives. Ask members how they sense the use of spiritual markers might help them in decision making. See if someone can give a personal example of how this process is helping them in a specific decision now.

2. Declare the wonderful works of the Lord (small group). Allow time for testimonies. Say: *If God has done something special in or through your life this week, please share what God has done so we can praise the Lord together.*

3. Focus on God (quads). Ask:

   a. What have you come to know about God, His purposes, or His ways in relationship to the church?

   b. What do you sense God wants our church to do in response to this knowledge of Him?

4. Most meaningful (quads). Ask members to review their five most meaningful statements or Scriptures for the unit (pp. 117, 120, 123, 127, and 130) and identify the one statement or Scripture that was the most meaningful of these five. Ask members to (a) read their most meaningful statements or Scriptures, (b) tell why they were meaningful, and (c) share how they responded to God in prayer.

5. Scripture memory (quads). Ask members to quote John 5:19 to one another and share what God may have said to them through this week's memory verse.

Prayer Time—15 minutes

1. Share requests (small group). Ask members to share concerns that have surfaced this week about your church or specific members in your church. Suggest that statements be specific and brief at this point so the group will have adequate time to pray.

2. Pray (quads). Divide into quads so members can be more actively involved in this prayer time. Ask members to pray specifically for your church and the church members mentioned in the previous sharing time.

3. Record prayer requests (small group). As groups finish praying, suggest: *Turn to the prayer section of your journal and record prayer requests or ways God led you to pray for our church or specific members of our church.*

Singing/Special Music—5 minutes

Optional special music (small group). Sing a hymn or chorus or play a recorded song that relates to God's speaking to and guiding His people. You might select songs like "All the Way My Savior Leads Me," "Guide Me, O Thou Great Jehovah," or "He Leadeth Me! O Blessed Thought."

Video Teaching Viewing and Discussion—45 minutes

1. View the video teaching for session 6 (small group). Invite members to turn to the viewer guide on page 131 and view session 6.

2. Discuss the message and testimony (small group). Ask and discuss the following questions or use your own.

    a. What is one of the most critical factors in coming to the point that you recognize God's voice?

    b. What are some factors to keep in mind when you face open and closed doors?

    c. What are some ways God speaks through circumstances and other believers? What examples from Richard's message can you give?

    d. How do the four ways we've seen God speaks—the Bible, prayer, circumstances, and other believers—work together?

3. Discussion (small group). Ask members to discuss the following: *What is the most meaningful thing you learned or reviewed during this message about God's speaking through circumstances and the church? How can the idea of identifying spiritual markers help you understand more clearly what God is doing in your life?*

Closure—5 minutes

1. Wait on the Lord (small group). Review any questions or concerns that may have come up during the session. Ask the group to pray for these concerns and seek answers to questions during the coming week.

2. Preview unit 7 (small group). Ask members to pay special attention to the four statements listed in "The Crisis of Belief" box on page 137. Ask members to write in the margins of their books any prayer concerns they think of as they study the next unit. If they have concerns about the way your church walks by faith, ask them to pray about them and not discuss them with anyone at this point. Explain that Henry had to spend time helping his church learn how to know God's will before members were ready to walk by faith in some of the ways described. The budgeting process described at the beginning of unit 7 may not be the way God calls your church to walk by faith. Encourage members to let God take the initiative in guiding your church in specific ways to walk by faith. Members should not try to force a method or a program on the rest of the church. That could be detrimental to the fellowship.

3. Pray (small group). Join hands in a circle and lead the closing prayer yourself. Ask God to teach all of you this week what walking by faith requires. Ask Him for patience as He guides your whole church to a deeper walk of faith.

The Crisis of Belief

1. An encounter with God requires faith.
2. Encounters with God are God-sized.
3. What you do in response to God's revelation (invitation) reveals what you believe about God.
4. True faith requires action.

AFTER THE SESSION

Use the standard guide on LG page 63 to evaluate the session.

THE CRISIS OF BELIEF

BEFORE THE SESSION

❑ 1. Complete all the learning activities in unit 7 of the member book.

❑ 2. Read again the caution in "Preview Unit 7" in the previous group session (LG p. 36). The reason I have given you this caution is that I have seen some pastors and some laypersons try to force this budgeting method on their church. Unless the proper foundation has been established so people know how to hear clearly when God is speaking, this method will not work. As Henry said, *"It* never works. *He* works." Try to help your group pray through any concerns they have about your church. As God leads your church to walk by faith, He will show you how to approach any change He may desire. Encourage members to be faithful and respond only to God's leading. His timing will always be right.

❑ 3. Pray now for God's guidance as you prepare for this group session. Pray specifically for each member of your group.

❑ 4. Read "During the Session." Select the activities that best suit the learning needs of your group. Adapt or develop other activities that you sense will best help your group gain the greatest benefit from the unit of study.

❑ 5. Decide on the amount of time to allow for each activity. Write a time in the margin to indicate when each activity should begin. Always be prepared to change your plans if the Holy Spirit leads you in another direction.

❑ 6. Gather the "Seven Realities" poster and any other items you need for activities you may have developed on your own.

❑ 7. Remove the unit posters from the previous session and save them for future use. Display the posters you have prepared for unit 7 (LG p. 9).

❑ 8. *Optional:* Select a hymn, chorus, or recorded song for use during the large group time.

❑ 9. Prepare a one-minute preview of unit 8.

❑ 10. If you are using the video teaching sessions, do the following.

• Secure and set up the equipment necessary for viewing.

• Preview the session 7 video teaching (16:59 min.) and list one or two key ideas or questions you think will be of special interest to your group members.

• Think about your own response to the video teaching discussion questions in "During the Session." Make your own list of possible commitments to planned obedience.

SESSION LEARNING OBJECTIVES

This session will help members—

• state and explain four principles related to the crisis of belief;

• define *faith* and identify the opposite of faith;

• distinguish between actions that indicate faith and those that indicate a lack of faith;

• demonstrate a willingness to encourage and guide your church to plan for obedience as the body of Christ.

DURING THE SESSION

Arrival Activity—5 minutes

1. Greet members as they arrive. Ask them to complete the unit review on page 153 while others are coming in and to make sure they have completed the learning activities that will be discussed in "Sharing Time."

2. Open with prayer (quads). Ask members to share with the others in the quad a way the group can pray for them. These requests may relate to church, family, personal, or work. Encourage members to make the requests brief so they will have time to pray. Ask the quads to pray for the requests mentioned.

Unit Review—15 minutes

1. Seven realities (small group). Call for a volunteer to explain the fifth reality of experiencing God. Then ask for a volunteer to use the "Seven Realities" poster and state at least the first five realities.

2. Review (small group). Review the four statements at the bottom of page 153 related to the crisis of belief. For each statement ask members either to state biblical support for the statement or to briefly explain what they learned about the particular subject.

3. Q & A (small group). As time permits, ask volunteers to answer the following.
   a. What is faith, and what is the opposite of faith (p. 138)?
   b. Why does God give God-sized assignments that are humanly impossible (day 3, pp. 142–45)?
   c. What is the relationship between faith and action (day 4, pp. 146–49)?
   d. According to Hebrews 11, can you determine a person's faith by the good or bad outcome in his life? Why or why not (p. 151)?

4. Case-study discussion (small group). Review each of the four case studies on pages 147–48 and ask members to discuss their responses to each one. Discuss those on which members have a difference of opinion. Make sure members base their answers on biblical truth and not just human experience. Gently call attention to any effort to base a response on experience alone.

5. Poster discussion (small group). Focus attention on the statements on the unit posters you have displayed. Read each statement and ask members to comment on what that statement means to them. Ask what adjustments may be needed in their lives to relate correctly to God.

Sharing Time—30 minutes

1. Written responses (small group). Ask members to turn in their books to the following learning activities and respond as indicated. Topics are listed in the "Sharing Time" box with the review.

   • Activities 4–7 on page 136. Compare your answers in activities 4 and 5 and discuss your responses to activities 6 and 7.
   • Times in your life when faith was required and how you responded (activities 3 and 4, p. 141)
   • Activity 4 on page 144. Compare your answers to items a–d. Share, compare, and discuss your responses to items e–h.
   • One of the most meaningful statements or Scriptures from this unit's lessons— choose one from pages 137, 141, 145, 150, and 152. Share the statement and your prayer response to God.

2. ***Declare the wonderful works of the Lord (small group).*** Allow time for testimonies. Say: *If God has done something special in or through your life this week, please share what God has done so we can praise the Lord together.*

3. ***Scripture memory (pairs).*** Ask members to quote Hebrews 11:6 to each other and share what God may have said to them through this week's memory verse.

4. ***Focus on God (quads).*** Ask:
   a. *What have you come to know about God, His purposes, or His ways this week?*
   b. *What do you sense God wants you to do in response to this knowledge of Him?*

Prayer Time—15 minutes

1. ***Share requests and pray (quads).*** (Use the same grouping formed in the opening prayer time.) Ask members to briefly share their concerns about walking by faith as individuals and as a church. Then ask members to pray specifically for one another and for your church.

2. ***Record prayer requests (small group).*** As groups finish praying, suggest: *Turn to the prayer section of your journal and record prayer requests or ways God led you to pray for the faith of other believers and for the faith of your church.*

Music—5 minutes

Optional special music (small group). Sing a hymn or chorus or play a recorded song that relates to faith and action like "Have Faith in God," "Trust, Try, and Prove Me," or "Faith Is the Victory." For special music you might consider playing a recording of "Find Us Faithful."

Video Teaching Viewing and Discussion—45 minutes

1. ***View the video teaching for session 7 (small group).*** Invite members to turn to the viewer guide on page 153 and view session 7.

2. ***Discuss the message and testimony (small group).*** Ask and discuss the following questions or use your own.
   a. *How does Mike's story about Richard taking him on a roller coaster as a young boy illustrate the nature of faith and a crisis of belief?*
   b. *What is the difference between a crisis and a crisis of belief?*
   c. *What are some examples of when our faith in Jesus will call us into action for Jesus?*

3. ***Apply the truth to your church.*** *What are some things you sense God is saying to your church? How do you think your church should respond?*

Closure—5 minutes

1. ***Wait on the Lord (small group).*** Review any questions or concerns that may have come up during the session. Ask the group to pray for these concerns and seek answers to questions during the coming week.

2. ***Preview unit 8 (small group).*** Ask members to pay special attention to the kinds of adjustments that may be required for a person to move into the mainstream of God's activity.

3. ***Pray (small group).*** Ask members to join hands in a circle and pray for your church and for one another as you regularly face the crisis of belief.

AFTER THE SESSION

Use the standard guide on LG page 63 to evaluate the session.

SESSION 8

ADJUSTING YOUR LIFE TO GOD

SESSION LEARNING OBJECTIVES

This session will help members—

- state six of the realities of experiencing God;
- identify ways a person waits on the Lord;
- identify ways God has led them to make adjustments in their lives;
- demonstrate a commitment to the lordship of Christ by verbalizing a prayer of surrender.

BEFORE THE SESSION

❑ 1. Complete all the learning activities in unit 8 of the member book.

❑ 2. Pray now for God's guidance as you prepare for this group session. Pray specifically for each member of your group.

❑ 3. Read "During the Session." Select the activities that best suit the learning needs of your group. Adapt or develop other activities you sense will best help your group gain the greatest benefit from the unit of study.

❑ 4. Decide on the amount of time to allow for each activity. Write a time in the margin to indicate when each activity should begin. Always be prepared to change your plans if the Holy Spirit leads you and the group in another direction.

❑ 5. Gather the following items and include any others you need for activities you may have developed on your own.
- The "Seven Realities" poster
- A dry-erase board or newsprint and suitable markers

❑ 6. Remove the unit posters from the previous session and save them for future use. Display the posters you have prepared for unit 8 (LG p. 9).

❑ 7. Prepare a one-minute preview of unit 9. Pay special attention to the additional instructions in "During the Session."

❑ 8. If you are using the video teaching, do the following.
- Secure and set up the equipment necessary for viewing.
- Preview the session 8 video teaching (15:13 min.) and list one or two key ideas or questions you think will be of special interest to your group members. Use these ideas to introduce the session's video teaching message.
- Think about your own response to the video teaching discussion questions in "During the Session." Think about how you will respond after "Prayer Time" if people have been deeply touched by the Lord.

DURING THE SESSION

Arrival Activity—5 minutes

1. Greet members as they arrive. Ask them to complete the unit review on page 177 while others are coming in and to make sure they have completed the learning activities that will be discussed in "Sharing Time."

2. Open with prayer (small group). Call on a member to pray and ask God to guide all group members to make the adjustments He desires of them.

Unit Review—15 minutes

1. Seven realities (small group). Display the "Seven Realities" poster. Point to the arrow at the top and ask a member to state the first reality. Turn to the next person in the circle and ask her to state the second reality. Continue around the circle until you have stated at least the first six. Mention that in the next unit members will study the seventh reality in detail.

2. Review (small group). Review and discuss, if needed, the answers to the questions on the unit review. Spend time discussing the written responses to the last two questions. Ask: *What does a person do while he is waiting on the Lord?* As members respond, write their responses on a dry-erase board or on newsprint. (Answer: pray, watch circumstances, share with and listen to other believers, continue doing the last thing God told you to do—p. 174)

3. Q & A (small group). As time permits, ask volunteers to answer the following.

  a. What is required as a demonstration of faith (p. 156)?

  b. Who are some of the people in the Bible who had to make adjustments to God, and what adjustments did they have to make (p. 157)?

  c. Who is one Bible character who was asked to make an adjustment but refused (p. 158)?

  d. What are some kinds of adjustments you may have to make in order to obey God (p. 160)?

  e. Does God ever ask a person to change his own plans and directions in order to follow God's purposes (pp. 164–65)? Do you think He will ever ask you to change your plans and directions in order to follow Him? (Note: if some answer no to this second question, remind them that they cannot stay where they are and go with God. God always requires an adjustment.)

4. Poster discussion (small group). Focus attention on the statements on the unit posters you have displayed. Read each statement and ask members to comment on what that statement means to them. Ask what adjustments may be needed in their lives to relate correctly to God.

Sharing Time—30 minutes

1. Scripture memory (pairs). Ask members to quote Luke 14:33 to each other and share what God may have said to them through this week's memory verse.

2. Written responses (quads). Ask members to turn in their books to the following learning activities and share responses with one another. Topics are listed in the "Sharing Time" box with the review.

  • One of the most meaningful statements or Scriptures from this unit's lessons and your prayer response to God. Choose one from pages 159, 163, 167, 171, and 176.

  • Adjustments you have made in your thinking during this course (p. 161)

  • The quotation on page 162 that was most meaningful and why

  • An experience that required costly adjustment or obedience (p. 166)

- How your church would be seen in regard to prayer and adjustments God may want your church to make (p. 176)
3. **Declare the wonderful works of the Lord (small group).** Allow time for testimonies. Say: *If God has done something special in or through your life this week, please share what God has done so we can praise the Lord together.*
4. **Focus on God (small group).** Ask:
    a. *What have you come to know about God, His purposes, or His ways this week?*
    b. *What do you sense God wants you to do in response to this knowledge of Him?*

Video Teaching Viewing and Discussion—45 minutes
1. **View the video teaching for session 8 (small group).** Invite members to turn to the viewer guide on page 177 and view session 8.
2. **Discuss the message and testimony (small group).** Ask and discuss the following questions or use your own.
    a. *How does making adjustments to God increase our faith and trust in His plans?*
    b. *What are some examples Mike shares of the kinds of adjustments that were required for him to obey the Lord? What are some things he would have missed if he had not made those adjustments?*

Prayer Time—15 minutes
1. **Sharing and recording prayer requests (small group).** Ask members to turn to the prayer-request section of their spiritual journals. Ask them to share specific requests they have about their prayer lives and the prayer life of your church.
2. **Pray (quads).** Ask members to pray conversationally for the requests just mentioned in the small group.

Closure—5 minutes
1. **Wait on the Lord (small group).** Review any questions or concerns that may have come up during the session. Ask the group to pray for these concerns and seek answers to questions during the coming week.
2. **Preview unit 9 (small group).** The next unit will focus on obedience. Some of your members will find this to be a very difficult study as they evaluate their own level of obedience. You will need to give them a word of encouragement. Read Matthew 28:18-20. Point out that one of the church's assignments is to help members obey. Mention that in the next session members will help, encourage, and pray for one another in the area of obedience.
3. **Pray (quads).** Ask members to join hands and pray about adjustments they sense they may need to make in response to God. Encourage members to surrender absolutely to Christ's lordship and to pray for one another as well. Tell them they are dismissed as they finish praying in their quads. Remind them to be quiet while others finish praying.

AFTER THE SESSION

Use the standard guide on LG page 63 to evaluate the session.

EXPERIENCING GOD THROUGH OBEDIENCE

BEFORE THE SESSION

❏ 1. Complete all the learning activities in unit 9 of the member book.

❏ 2. Pray now for God's guidance as you prepare for this group session. Pray specifically for each member of your group.

❏ 3 Read "During the Session." Select the activities that best suit the learning needs of your group. Adapt or develop other activities you sense will best help your group gain the greatest benefit from the unit of study.

❏ 4. Decide on the amount of time to allow for each activity. Write a time in the margin to indicate when each activity should begin. Always be prepared to change your plans if the Holy Spirit leads you and the group in another direction.

❏ 5. Gather the following items and any other items you need for activities you may have developed on your own.
   • The "Seven Realities" poster
   • A dry-erase board or newsprint and suitable markers

❏ 6. Remove the unit posters from the previous session and save them for future use. Display the posters you have prepared for unit 9 (LG p. 9).

❏ 7. *Optional:* Select a hymn, chorus, or recorded song for use during the large group time.

❏ 8. Prepare a one-minute preview of unit 10. Prepare to encourage members to pray especially for your church this week.

❏ 9. If you are using the video teaching, do the following.
   • Secure and set up the equipment for viewing.
   • Preview the session 9 video teaching (15:14 min.) and list one or two key ideas or questions you think will be of special interest to your group members. Use these ideas to introduce the video teaching.
   • Think about your own response to the video teaching discussion questions in "During the Session."

SESSION LEARNING OBJECTIVES

This session will help members—
• state all seven of the realities of experiencing God in order;
• identify the importance and meaning of obedience;
• explain why Christian maturity is often a slow process;
• demonstrate their worship of God by sharing ways they have personally experienced God.

DURING THE SESSION

Psalm 119:33-35

"Teach [us], O LORD, to follow
your decrees; then [we]
will keep them to the end.
Give [us] understanding,
and [we] will keep your
law and obey it with all
[our] heart.
Direct [us] in the path of
your commands, for there
[we] find delight."

Arrival Activity—5 minutes

1. Greet members as they arrive. Ask them to complete the unit review on page 197 while others are coming in and to make sure they have completed the learning activities that will be discussed in "Sharing Time."

2. Open with prayer (small group). Paraphrase Psalm 119:33-35 (p. 182) to become a group prayer by using *us*, *we*, and *our* instead of *I*, *me*, and *my*. Ask group members to express their agreement with this prayer by praying in unison, "We love You, Lord, so we will obey You."

Unit Review—15 minutes

1. Seven realities (pairs). Ask members to state the seven realities in order to their partners. Display the "Seven Realities" poster in case a person needs the diagram as a prompt.

2. God's pattern (small group). Remind the group that these are not steps or a method to follow. These seven statements describe God's pattern of working with His people. He always takes the initiative. We do not take the initiative in accomplishing God's purposes. Say: *We have studied these seven realities of God so you will be able to identify God's activity in your life. Now when God takes the initiative to involve you in His work, I trust that you will know how to respond to Him by acting in faith, making the necessary adjustments, and obeying Him.*

3. Q & A (small group). Move through as many of the following questions as time allows.

    a. How important is obedience (p. 182)?

    b. What is the meaning of obedience (pp. 183–84)?

    c. When a person disobeys God, does God give him or her a second chance? Explain your answer (pp. 185–86).

    d. Why does God sometimes work slowly in a person's life to bring the person to maturity (p. 192)?

    e. Write responses to the following on a dry-erase board or newsprint. What are some of the things you would do when faced with a circumstance that seemed to close the door on God's will (p. 194)?

4. Poster discussion (small group). Focus attention on the statements on the unit posters you have displayed. Read each statement and ask members to comment on what that statement means to them. Ask what adjustments may be needed in their lives to relate correctly to God.

Sharing Time—30 minutes

1. Scripture memory (pairs). Ask members to quote John 14:23 to each other and share what God may have said to them through this week's memory verse.

2. Written responses (pairs). Ask members to turn in their books to the following learning activities and share responses with each other. Topics are listed in the "Sharing Time" box with the review.

- Statements that have influenced the way you love and obey God (p. 180)
- Activity 4 on page 184
- Statements that have been meaningful to you (p. 188)
- Names by which you have come to know God by experience (p. 191)
- One of the most meaningful statements or Scriptures from this unit's lessons and your prayer response to God. Choose one from pages 183, 187, 190, and 196.

3. Focus on God (small group). Ask:

    a. *What have you come to know about God, His purposes, or His ways this week?*

    b. *What do you sense God wants you to do in response to this knowledge of Him?*

4. Declare the wonderful works of the Lord (small group). Allow time for testimonies. Say: *If God has done something special in or through your life this week, please share what God has done so we can praise the Lord together.*

Prayer Time—15 minutes

1. Share requests and pray (pairs). Ask members to share with their partners one area of obedience they presently struggle with or one act of obedience they know God is guiding them to do. Then ask members to pray for their partners and their specific need in the area of obedience.

2. Record prayer requests (small group). As pairs finish praying, suggest: *Turn to the prayer section of your journal and record prayer requests or ways God led you to pray for your partner.*

Singing/Special Music—5 minutes

Optional special music (small group). Sing a hymn or chorus or play a recorded song that relates to obedience or experiencing God at work. Use songs like "Trust and Obey," "Living for Jesus," or "Make Me a Channel of Blessing."

Video Teaching Viewing and Discussion—45 minutes

1. View the video teaching for session 9 (small group). Invite members to turn to the viewer guide on page 197 and view session 9.

2. Discuss the message and testimony (small group). Ask and discuss the following questions or use your own.

    a. *How did Richard's story about Mike playing with neighborhood boys illustrate God the Father's desire for us to obey Him as His children?*

    b. *What truths about obedience have you heard that help you understand the place and importance of obedience?*

    c. *What are some possible but inadequate substitutes for obedience?*

Closure—5 minutes

1. Wait on the Lord (small group). Review any questions or concerns that may have come up during the session. Ask the group to pray for these concerns and seek answers to questions during the coming week.

2. Preview unit 10 (small group). Ask members to pay special attention to the way a church comes to understand and do God's will.

3. Pray (small group). Ask volunteers to pray prayers of commitment to the absolute lordship of Christ. After several have prayed, close by asking God to teach all of you, during the coming unit, how to know and do His will as a church.

AFTER THE SESSION

Use the standard guide on LG page 63 to evaluate the session.

SESSION 10

GOD'S WILL AND THE CHURCH

BEFORE THE SESSION

SESSION LEARNING OBJECTIVES

This session will help members—

• identify biblical concerns God has for His churches;

• distinguish between the way churches and individuals come to know the will of God;

• apply biblical instructions for churches to their church life together;

• demonstrate love for their church by praying for it and its leaders.

❑ 1. Complete all the learning activities in unit 10 of the member book.

❑ 2. Pray now for God's guidance as you prepare for this group session. Pray specifically for each member of your group. Pray for your church. Pray that this group session will be a significant time of growth for your members as they focus on Christ as the Head of His church.

❑ 3. Read "During the Session." Select the activities that best suit the learning needs of your group. Adapt or develop other activities you sense will best help your group gain the greatest benefit from the unit of study.

❑ 4. Decide on the amount of time to allow for each activity. Write a time in the margin to indicate when each activity should begin. Always be prepared to change your plans if the Holy Spirit leads you and the group in another direction.

❑ 5. Remove the unit posters from the previous session and save them for future use. Display the posters you have prepared for unit 10 (LG p. 9).

❑ 6. *Optional:* Select a hymn, chorus, or recorded song for use during the large group time.

❑ 7. Prepare a one-minute preview of unit 11.

❑ 8. If you are using the video teaching sessions, do the following.
   • Secure and set up the equipment for viewing.
   • Preview the session 10 video teaching (17:42 min.) and list one or two key ideas or questions you think will be of special interest to your group members. Use these ideas to introduce the video teaching message.
   • Think about your own response to the video teaching discussion questions in "During the Session."

DURING THE SESSION

Arrival Activity—5 minutes

1. *Greet members as they arrive.* Ask them to complete the unit review on page 223 while others are coming in and to make sure they have completed the learning activities that will be discussed in "Sharing Time."

2. *Open with prayer (small group).* Ask a member to pray that God will use this session to help group members and your church mature as a healthy body of Christ.

Unit Review—15 minutes

1. *Review (small group).* Review and discuss, if needed, the three concerns God has for the body of Christ in the review on page 223. You will discuss responses to the last two questions in the review during "Sharing Time."

2. *Q & A (small group).* As time permits, ask volunteers to answer the following.
   a. *What is the difference between the way an individual comes to know God's will and the way a church does (p. 203)?*
   b. *When are some times that members of a church body could share with others what they sense God wants the church to be and do (p. 204)?*
   c. *How did you describe our church's decision-making process on page 205?*
   d. *Who is responsible for convincing a church what God's will is and when the church should do it (p. 206)?*
   e. *What is a good question to use in a church business meeting to discern God's will rather than human opinion (p. 207)?*
   f. *What is a spiritual gift (p. 211)?*
   g. *What are some biblical principles for the way a church ought to function as a body (p. 214)?*
   h. *What does the Bible say God's will is for relationships in the church body (p. 219)?*

3. *Poster discussion (small group).* Focus attention on the statements on the unit posters you have displayed. Read each statement and ask members to comment on what that statement means to them. Ask what adjustments may be needed in their lives to relate correctly to God.

Sharing Time—30 minutes

1. *Written responses (small group).* Ask members to turn to the following learning activities and share responses with one another. Topics are listed in the "Sharing Time" box with the review.
   • What you sense God is saying about the way our church makes decisions (p. 209)
   • The last two questions in the unit review
   • Things that might help you function more effectively in the body (p. 216)
   • Activity 5 on page 217
   • Instructions from Romans 12 and 1 Corinthians 12 for your church and for you (pp. 210 and 220)
   • One of the most meaningful statements or Scriptures from this unit and your prayer response to God (pp. 204, 209, 212, 217, and 222)

2. *Focus on God (pairs).* Ask:
   a. *What have you come to know about God, His purposes, or His ways this week?*
   b. *What do you sense God wants you to do in response to this knowledge of Him?*

3. *Declare the wonderful works of the Lord (small group).* Allow time for testimonies. Say: *If God has done something special in or through your life this week, please share what God has done so we can praise the Lord together.*

4. Scripture memory (quads). Ask members to quote Romans 12:5 to one another and share what God may have said to them through this week's memory verse.

Prayer Time—15 minutes

1. Share requests and pray (quads). Ask members to share concerns they have for your church. Then ask them to pray that God will convince all of your church about what His will is, regardless of human desires.

2. Record prayer requests (small group). As groups finish praying, suggest: *Turn to the prayer section of your journal and record prayer requests or ways God led you to pray for our church.*

Singing/Special Music—5 minutes

Optional special music (small group). Sing a hymn or chorus or play a recorded song that relates to the church, such as "The Church's One Foundation," "Break Out, O Church of God," "God Still Moves," "We Are One in the Bond of Love," "Bind Us Together," or "The Family of God." Consider playing a recording of "The Church Triumphant."

Video Teaching Viewing and Discussion—45 minutes

1. View the video teaching for session 10 (small group). Invite members to turn to the viewer guide on page 223 and view session 10.

2. Discuss the message and testimony (small group). Ask and discuss the following questions or use your own.

   a. In a world that is very individualistic, why do we need the community of the church?

   b. What truths about the body of Christ have you heard that you would most like to experience?

   c. What do you believe God is saying to you about your role in the body of Christ? What are some ways you sense our church could function more closely as the body of Christ?

Closure—5 minutes

1. Wait on the Lord (small group). Review any questions or concerns that may have come up during the session. Ask the group to pray for these concerns and seek answers to questions during the coming week.

2. Preview unit 11 (small group). Ask members to pay special attention to what they learn from First John about the way relationships with our Christian brothers and sisters indicate the quality and depth of our relationship with God.

3. Pray (small group). Ask members to pray conversationally for your church and your church's leaders that God would help all of you function more effectively as the body of Christ.

AFTER THE SESSION

Use the standard guide on LG page 63 to evaluate the session.

KINGDOM PEOPLE

BEFORE THE SESSION

❑ 1. Complete all the learning activities in unit 11 in the member book.

❑ 2. Pray now for God's guidance as you prepare for this group session. Pray specifically for each member of your group.

❑ 3. Read "During the Session." Select the activities that best suit the learning needs of your group. Adapt or develop other activities you sense will best help your group gain the greatest benefit from the unit of study.

❑ 4. Decide on the amount of time to allow for each activity. Write a time in the margin to indicate when each activity should begin. Always be prepared to change your plans if the Holy Spirit leads you and the group in another direction.

❑ 5. Gather the following item and any other items you need for activities you may have developed on your own.
   • *Optional:* One copy of *"Experiencing God* Course Evaluation" for each member (download and print the file *EG_Evaluation.pdf* available at lifeway.com/egleader)

❑ 6. Remove the unit posters from the previous session and save them for future use. Display the posters you have prepared for unit 11 (LG p. 9).

❑ 7. Prepare a one-minute preview of unit 12.

❑ 8. If you are using the video teaching sessions, do the following.
   • Secure and set up the equipment necessary for viewing.
   • Preview the session 11 video teaching (12:32 min.) and list one or two key ideas or questions you think will be of special interest to your group members. Use these ideas to introduce the video teaching.
   • Think about your own response to the video teaching discussion questions in "During the Session." Think about how you will respond after "Prayer Time" if people have been deeply touched by the Lord.

SESSION LEARNING OBJECTIVES

This session will help members—

• identify ways a local church can be a world-missions strategy center;

• apply Kingdom principles and truths to your church;

• define *koinonia* and explain ways it can be reflected in relationships with other Christians and churches;

• write and explain the application of four essentials of koinonia;

• demonstrate a desire for the full expression of *koinonia* in your church by praying for your church and by taking an action that will enhance *koinonia*.

DURING THE SESSION

Arrival Activity—5 minutes

1. Greet members as they arrive. Ask them to complete the unit review on page 247 while others are coming in and to make sure they have completed the learning activities that will be discussed in the "Sharing Time."

2. Open with prayer (small group). Lead in a prayer for guidance that your church truly might become a world-missions strategy center.

Unit Review—15 minutes

1. Q & A (small group). As time permits, ask volunteers to answer the following.

a. *How can a local church be a world-missions strategy center (pp. 226–28)?*

b. *What is koinonia (p. 229)?*

c. *What is love as described in 1 Corinthians 13? And what is love not (p. 232)?*

d. *How will people know that we are disciples of Jesus (John 13:35 and p. 232)?*

e. *What are ways* koinonia *can be reflected in relationships between churches (pp. 234–38)?*

f. *What are the four essentials of* koinonia *and how would a church function to maintain each of these essentials (pp. 240–46)?*

g. *What are some things that can threaten or compete with your love for God (p. 240)?*

h. *How does interference with Christ's rule threaten* koinonia *in a church (pp. 241–42)?*

i. *What are some things that happen in a church that can take the place of a real and personal encounter with God (p. 244)?*

j. *What are some things or people in which church members may be tempted to place their trust (p. 245)?*

2. Poster discussion (small group). Focus attention on the statements on the unit posters you have displayed. Read each statement and ask members to comment on what that statement means to them. Ask what adjustments may be needed in their lives to relate correctly to God.

Sharing Time—20 minutes

1. World-missions strategy center (small group). Ask members to turn to page 228.

• Ask: *What do you sense God is doing or wants to do to use our church as a world-missions strategy center?*

• Ask: *Has God added members to our body whom He wants to use to touch our world for Christ? If so, who? How?*

If God calls specific individuals to mind during this time of sharing, enlist members of the group to call them this week and ask probing questions (see p. 84) to learn whether God is already at work in their lives and now wants to involve the rest of the church with them.

2. Written responses (pairs). Ask members to turn to the following learning activities and share responses with each other. Topics are listed in the "Sharing Time" in the bottom right margin on page 247.

• The last three questions in the unit review

• One of the most meaningful statements or Scriptures from this unit's lessons and your prayer response to God. Choose one from pages 229, 233, 239, 242, and 246.

3. Scripture memory (pairs). Ask members to quote 1 John 1:7 to each other and share what God may have said to them through this week's memory verse.

4. Focus on God (small group). Ask:
  a. *What have you come to know about God, His purposes, or His ways this week?*
  b. *What do you sense God wants you to do in response to this knowledge of Him?*

5. Declare the wonderful works of the Lord (small group). Allow time for testimonies. Say: *If God has done something special in or through your life this week, please share what God has done so we can praise the Lord together.*

Video Teaching Viewing and Discussion—45 minutes

1. View the video teaching for session 11 (small group). Invite members to turn to the viewer guide on page 247 and view session 11.

2. Discuss the message and testimony (small group). Ask and discuss the following questions or use your own.
  a. *Why is it essential to be aware of the work God is doing in and through other people in your community and around the world?*
  b. *What truths about God's kingdom have your heard that reveal what God wants to do in our world?*
  c. *What are some characteristics of a healthy Kingdom citizen? What would he or she do?*

Prayer Time—15 minutes

1. Share requests and pray (small group). Rather than take time to hear requests, ask members to pray aloud for the prayer concerns that have grown from their study this week. The prayers may focus on the members' personal response to God and other Christians, or they may relate to your church and its response to God's kingdom principles.

2. Record prayer requests (small group). After the group finishes, suggest: *Turn to the prayer section of your journal and record prayer requests or ways God led you to pray for yourself or for our church.*

Closure—10 minutes

1. Wait on the Lord (small group). Review any questions or concerns that may have come up during the session. Ask the group to pray for these concerns and seek answers to questions this week.

2. Preview unit 12 (small group). Ask members to pay special attention to the essentials of maintaining *koinonia.*

3. Course evaluation (small group). If you decided to request an evaluation of the course, distribute copies of *"Experiencing God* Course Evaluation." Ask members to place this in their books at the beginning of unit 12. Ask them to complete the evaluation for your benefit, so that you will learn how to improve the small group experience next time you lead this study. Mention that they do not have to write their names on them. Tell them you will collect the evaluations at the next session.

4. Set a date (small group). Ask members to bring their calendars to the next session or check available dates four to six weeks away. Explain that in the next group session you will decide on a possible date for an informal get-together to give out diplomas and spend time sharing and praying together.

5. Pray (small group). Ask a member to pray that your church will experience all the dimensions of *koinonia* that God wants for it and that it truly will be a world-missions strategy center.

AFTER THE SESSION

Use the standard guide on LG page 63 to evaluate the session.

SESSION 12

EXPERIENCING GOD IN YOUR DAILY LIFE

SESSION LEARNING OBJECTIVES

This session will help members—

- identify evidences of a departure from intimacy with God and determine God's remedy;
- identify ways to join God's activity in their spouses' lives;
- identify ways to join God's activity in their children's lives;
- identify ways they can encourage other Christians to love and good deeds;
- demonstrate their commitment to continue experiencing God in their daily lives.

BEFORE THE SESSION

❏ 1. Complete all the learning activities in unit 12 of the member book.

❏ 2. Pray now for God's guidance as you prepare for this group session. Pray specifically for each member of your group.

❏ 3. Read "During the Session." Select the activities that best suit the learning needs of your group. Adapt or develop other activities you sense will best help your group gain the greatest benefit from the unit of study.

❏ 4. Decide on the amount of time to allow for each activity. Write a time in the margin to indicate when each activity should begin. Always be prepared to change your plans if the Holy Spirit leads you and the group in another direction.

❏ 5. Gather the following items and any other items you need for activities you may have developed on your own.
   - A dry-erase board or newsprint and suitable markers
   - Extra copies of the course-evaluation form distributed last week for members who forget to return theirs

❏ 6. Remove the unit posters from the previous session and save them for future use. Display the posters you have prepared for unit 12 (LG p. 9).

❏ 7. If you did not enlist help during session 11, call and enlist members to bring light refreshments for the break period.

❏ 8. Contact the church office or the appropriate person and check the church calendar for possible dates for your final get-together. Checking with the church will enable you to avoid any conflicts with other events that might involve your small group members.

❏ 9. If you are using the video teaching sessions, do the following:
   - Secure and set up the equipment necessary for viewing.
   - Preview the session 12 video teaching (20:56 min.) and list one or two key ideas or questions you think will be of special interest to your group members. Use these ideas to introduce the video teaching.
   - Think about your own response to the video teaching discussion questions in "During the Session." Think about how you will respond after "Prayer Time" if people have been deeply touched by the Lord.

❏ 10. Discuss with your church's discipleship-training director (or the person responsible for planning discipleship courses) to find out when another study of *Experiencing God* will be offered. Also find out what future training opportunities have already been scheduled so you can share this information with your group in the next session. Prepare a copy of these scheduled training events for each member, or you may want to write them on a poster for display.

During the Session **Arrival Activity**—5 minutes

1. Greet members as they arrive. Encourage them to work with a partner and complete the unit review on page 267. Ask them to be sure they have completed the learning activities that will be discussed in "Sharing Time." Collect completed copies of the course evaluation that you distributed in the previous session. If members have not completed theirs, ask them to finish while others arrive.

2. Opening prayer (small group). Call on a member to begin the session with a prayer of thanksgiving for the *koinonia* God has developed in the group.

Unit Review—15 minutes

1. Q &A (small group). As time permits, ask volunteers to answer some of the following:

   a. *What are some evidences that you have departed from your intimacy with God (activity 1, p. 250)?*

   b. *What are some ways you can join God's activity in your spouse's life (pp. 255–56)?*

   c. *What are some ways you can join God's activity in your children's lives (pp. 259–61)?*

   d. *What are some ways your church could encourage your Christian influence in your workplace and that of others (see day 4, pp. 261–64)?*

   e. *What are some things you can do to increase the likelihood that you will continue to experience God (pp. 265–66)?*

Sharing Time—30 minutes

1. Scripture memory (pairs). Ask members to quote Hebrews 10:24-25 to each other and share what God may have said to them through this week's memory verse. Ask: *What are some ways we can "spur one another on toward love and good deeds"?*

2. Written responses (small group). You will need plenty of time for the very important prayer time that follows this activity (LG p. 54). Limit the sharing of written responses to the time you have available. If necessary, stop this activity before all are finished so you will have adequate time to pray for one another. Ask members to turn in their books to the following learning activities and share responses with one another. Topics are listed in the "Sharing Time" box with the review.

   • One of the most meaningful statements or Scriptures from this unit's lessons and your prayer response to God. Choose one from pages 252, 257, 261, and 264.

   • How you would evaluate your intimacy with God (p. 250)

   • What you sense you should do next (p. 265)

Video Teaching Viewing and Discussion—45 minutes

1. View session 12 (small group). Invite members to turn to the listening guide on page 267 and view session 12.

2. Discuss the message and testimony (small group). Ask and discuss the following questions or use your own.

   a. *How did Mike's wife being led by God to bake bread for their church family lead to multiple opportunities for ministry?*

   b. *What have the truths or illustrations about experiencing God with your family or in your workplace inspired you to consider doing with your family or in your workplace?*

Prayer Time—15 minutes

1. Share requests and pray (quads or small group). Ask members to respond to this question:

> *What is the most meaningful thing we could pray*
> *about for your spiritual growth and walk with the Lord?*

After one person shares, ask the other members of the quad to stand around the person and pray for his or her request. Some members may want to place their hands on the shoulders of the person to express their support as they pray. After praying for this person, ask a second person to share. Then pray for him. Continue until all members have been prayed for.

Closure—5 minutes

1. Set a date (small group). Select a date for your final get-together.

2. Pray (small group). Stand in a circle and join hands. Close with a period of thanksgiving to God for all the wonderful things He has done during this course of study. Ask members to pray about one thanksgiving at a time, but encourage them to pray as many times as they want.

AFTER THE SESSION

1. Add to your spiritual journal a final list of specific ways you want to continue praying for group members and for your church.

2. Provide a final get-together for your group. Plan a cookout, a covered-dish meal, or a dinner at a local restaurant. Involve the group members in planning and preparing for the event. Mail invitations or call members to remind them of the date and time. At the meal ask members to give an update on what God is currently doing in their lives. Allow members to share up-to-date prayer requests on assignments they sense God has given or on adjustments they are making. Close the session with a time of conversational prayer as members pray for one another.

3. Take some time, perhaps on a personal half-day retreat, to evaluate your group study of *Experiencing God*. Use the following questions to start your thinking. Make notes for yourself on this page or in your journal. Begin your evaluation with a time of prayer for God's perspective.

    • How has God used this course and small group study to influence or improve your relationship with Him?

    • What has God done in the life of your church as a result of this study?

    • How have the spiritual leaders of your church responded to the changes in the members who have studied with you?

    • What do you think was the most meaningful experience during the study?

- What would you do differently in a future study of the course? (Consider things such as enlistment of participants, size of group, meeting time and place, learning activities, prayer times, and other details.)
- What should you do next? Lead another group? Study or teach another course? Begin or facilitate a new ministry?
  Complete the previous personal review before you proceed.

4. Review group members' responses to *"Experiencing God* Course Evaluation." Make summary notes on the things you think you would change with the next small group you lead through this study.

5. Gather the following materials and store them for use with future small group studies of *Experiencing God*.
   - The "Memorizing Scripture" poster
   - The "Seven Realities" poster
   - The "God Speaks Through the Bible" and "God Speaks Through Prayer" posters
   - The unit posters from units 1–12
   - Components of the leader kit
   - Notes you may have written that are not included in this leader guide
   - Other materials you prepared for group sessions

6. Spend a period in prayer and fellowship with God thanking Him for all He has done in and through your life and in your church during the past 13 weeks.

7. If God has done something that you sense is very significant in the life of your church as a result of this study, consider sharing a brief testimony with us. Write or type a one-page testimony on 8½-by-11-inch paper describing what God has done. On the back of the page include the following information.
   - Your name, address, and phone number
   - Your church's name, address, and phone number
   - Your pastor's name

Though we will be unable to acknowledge the many responses, we would like to hear about and keep a record of some of the wonderful works of our Lord God. Please mail the testimony to:

Experiencing God Editor
Adult Ministry Publishing
Lifeway Christian Resources
One Lifeway Plaza
Nashville, TN 37234-0152

NOTES

NOTES

NOTES

NOTES

NOTES

EXPERIENCING GOD WORKSHEET 1
JESUS' EXAMPLE

Read John 5:17,19-20 below and answer the questions that follow.

"My Father is still working, and I am working also. Truly I tell you, the Son is not able to do anything on his own, but only what he sees the Father doing. For whatever the Father does, the Son likewise does these things. 20 For the Father loves the Son and shows him everything he is doing, and he will show him greater works than these so that you will be amazed." (John 5:17,19-20, CSB).

1. Who is always at work? _____

2. How much can the Son do by Himself? _____

3. What does the Son do? _____

_____

4. Why does the Father show the Son what He is doing? _____

_____

This is one of the clearest statements of how Jesus knew what to do. Here is an outline of Jesus' approach to knowing and doing God's will:

JESUS' EXAMPLE

- The Father has been working right up until now.
- Now God has Me working.
- I do nothing on My own initiative.
- I watch to see what the Father is doing.
- The Father love Me.
- He shows Me everything He is doing.

EXPERIENCING GOD WORKSHEET 2
SEVEN REALITIES

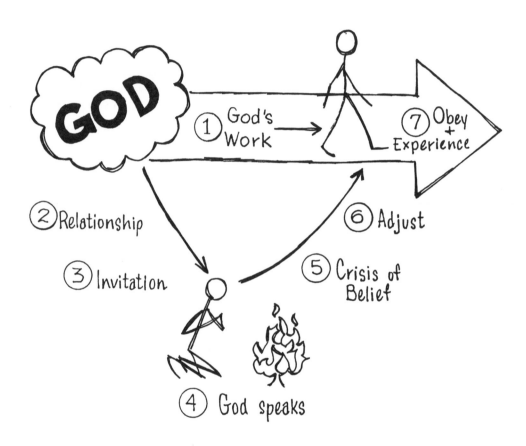

1. God is always at work around you.
2. God pursues a continuing love relationship with you that is real and personal.
3. God invites you to become involved with Him in His work.
4. God speaks by the Holy Spirit through the Bible, prayer, circumstances, and the church to reveal Himself, His purposes, and His ways.
5. God's invitation for you to work with Him always leads you to a crisis of belief that requires faith and action.
6. You must make major adjustments in your life to join God in what He is doing.
7. You come to know God by experience as you obey Him, and He accomplishes His work through you.

STANDARD DIRECTIONS FOR "AFTER THE SESSION"

Consider taking the following steps after each group session. Write notes as needed on separate paper or in your spiritual journal.

1. Record in your spiritual journal specific ways you can pray for group members. Do you sense a need to pray intently for any one person in particualar? If so, record concerns you need to pray about for that person.

2. Ask yourself the following questions and write notes on separate paper, on a prayer list, or in your spiritual journal:

   • What spiritual or mental preparation do I need to make for the next session that may have been lacking this week?

   • Which of the members need to be encouraged to participate more in the sharing and discussion times? When and how will I encourage them?

   • When could I have responded more appropriately to the needs of members or to the leadership of the Holy Spirit?

   • How well did I begin and end on time?

   • Which member most needs a call or note this week for encouragement, prayer, instruction, correction, or counsel? When shall I call or write?

3. Read "Before the Session" for next week's session to learn the preparation required for your next group session.

KEEP GROWING AS A DISCIPLE

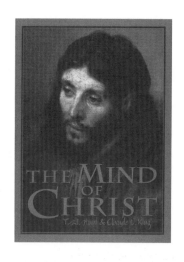

THE MIND OF CHRIST

T. W. Hunt and Claude V. King

Based on Philippians 2:5-11, this study teaches believers how to think the thoughts of Christ—to have the mind of Christ. T.W. Hunt brings thorough scriptural scholarship to his practical teachings on freedom in Christ, becoming like Christ, Christ's lifestyle, the servant mind, the glory of humanity, Christ's conduct among humans, living in the Spirit, the poles of holiness and love, the crucifixion, the resurrection, and the kingdom within.

Bible study book, ITEM 005173965
Viewer guide, ITEM 005174508
eBook and video sessions available
  at lifeway.com/themindofchrist

Spanish Bible study book,
  ITEM 001117224
Spanish leader guide, ITEM 001117224
Korean edition, ITEM 001117224

FRESH ENCOUNTER

Henry and Richard Blackaby and Claude V. King

Revival is needed in the church today, and our culture desperately needs a spiritual awakening. This study will bring you face-to-face with the truth of Scripture and the conviction of the Holy Spirit as you are called to return to God. You will also learn how God wants to use you as a catalyst for revival and spiritual awakening in your community and your world.

Bible study book, ITEM 005189421

eBook, video sessions, and audio sessions
  available at lifeway.com/freshencounter

To order, write to Lifeway Resources Customer Service; One Lifeway Plaza; Nashville, TN 37234-0113; email orderentry@lifeway.com; fax 615-251-5933; phone toll free 800-458-2772; order online at Lifeway.com.